EASY DOES
COOK IT BOOK

A FIVE (OR LESS) INGREDIENT COOKBOOK

Printed in the USA

ISBN #0-934474-60-5

TABLE OF CONTENTS

FAVORITE RECIPES
FROM MY COOKBOOK

Recipe Name	Page Number

APPETIZERS, BEVERAGES

COCKTAIL PIGS IN BLANKET

4 lb. cocktail sausage
2 recipes any biscuit
  dough

Cut dough in strips. Roll around sausage. Bake until brown; serve.

SWEET 'N SOUR WIENER BITES

1 (10 oz.) jar currant
  jelly
1 (6 oz.) jar prepared
  mustard
1 lb. Smokies cocktail
  wieners

Mix jelly and mustard in a chafing dish or double boiler. Heat, but do not boil. Add cocktail wieners to heated sauce and keep hot.

BACON-SOUR CREAM ROLL-UPS

1 pkg. crescent rolls
½ c. sour cream
½ lb. cooked bacon,
  crisp and
  crumbled
Dash of garlic powder

Mix the sour cream, crumbled bacon, and garlic powder. Chill at least 1 to 2 hours. Separate crescent rolls into 4 rectangles. Spread chilled mixture into rectangles. Roll up, starting with long end. Slice each into 6 pieces. Stand up (cut edge up and down) on baking sheet. Bake at 375° for 11 to 13 minutes. Serve warm.

HAM ROLL-UPS

1 (3 oz.) pkg. cream
  cheese
2 oz. shredded
  Cheddar cheese
½ tsp. prepared
  mustard
4 slices fully cooked
  ham
1 Tbsp. chopped
  green onion

Microwave cream cheese in small bowl at HIGH (100%) until softened, 10 to 15 seconds. Stir in Cheddar cheese, green onion, and mustard. Spread cheese mixture on ham slices. Roll ham from narrow end. Cut each roll into 4 pieces; secure with wooden pick. Place on paper toweling on carousel or large dinner plate. Microwave at HIGH (100%) 45 seconds to 1 minute and 30 seconds. Rotate plate half turn after half the time.

LIZ'S BACON WRAP-UPS

10 slices bread
15 slices bacon
1 c. cream of
  mushroom
  soup

Remove crusts from bread. Cut in 3 strips. Spread generously with undiluted mushroom soup (each bread strip). Cut bacon in halves. Place ½ slice of bacon under bread (not the soup side). Wrap as tightly as possible. Secure with a toothpick. Bake in jelly roll pan at 300° for 45 to 60 minutes. Makes 33.

May be made and frozen (before cooking).

BAJA BISCUIT BITES

1 (10 oz.) can
  refrigerated
  biscuits
6 oz. hickory smoked
  turkey breast or turkey
  ham
1 (4 oz.) can diced
  green chiles
4 (1 oz.) slices sharp
  American process
  cheese

Separate biscuit dough into 10 pieces. Gently flatten each piece of dough. Using a 1½ inch scalloped edge cookie cutter, cut 2 circles from each piece; roll again leftover dough and cut additional circles until all dough is used. Place dough circles on ungreased cookie sheet. Arrange turkey, green chiles, and ¼ slice of cheese on half of the circles. Bake at 400°F. for 8 to 10 minutes or until lightly browned. Place plain circles on top of filling before serving to make small biscuit "sandwiches."

YUMMY HOT DOGS

1 pkg. refrigerated
  crescent rolls
4 tsp. melted butter
  or margarine
4 tsp. prepared
  mustard
8 wieners
Sesame seeds

Separate crescents into 8 rolls. Brush each with melted butter and spread with mustard. Place wiener on wide end and roll toward narrow end. Place on ungreased baking sheet. Brush with melted butter and sprinkle with sesame seeds. Bake at 375° for 12 to 14 minutes or until rolls are lightly browned.

CRUNCHY CHEESE TIDBITS

1 c. butter
2 c. grated cheese
2 c. flour
2 c. Rice Krispies
  cereal

Mix all ingredients, *except* Rice Krispies. When well blended, gently stir in cereal. Roll small balls of the dough (about ½ inch) between hands until smooth.

STUFFED EGGS

1 egg, hard cooked
1 tsp. mustard
 (prepared)
Salt and pepper to
 taste
Paprika (optional)

Cut egg in half lengthwise and scoop out the yolk without breaking the white. Cream the yolks with a fork and mix with mustard and salt and pepper. Return yolk to hollow part of the white and sprinkle with paprika.

PARMESAN ONION CANAPES

1 c. Hellmann's mayo
1 c. grated Parmesan
 cheese
½ c. onion, finely
 chopped
1 Tbsp. milk
1 loaf sliced cocktail
 bread

Mix first 4 ingredients. Lightly toast bread. Spread mixture on toast. Place 4 inches from broiler and broil 2 to 3 minutes.

NACHOS

Large size plain or
 taco flavored
 tortilla corn chips
1 (10½ oz.) can Fritos
 jalapeno bean
 dip
Grated Cheddar
 cheese

Mound about a teaspoon of bean dip on each tortilla corn chip. Top with grated cheese. Place on paper plate and cook in microwave oven approximately 30 seconds. Or place on baking sheet and bake at 350° until cheese is melted. Serve hot.

Tip: Do not prepare ahead of time. The bean mixture tends to soften the corn chips and make them tough instead of crisp.

HIDDEN VALLEY RANCH CHEESE FINGERS

2 small loaves French
 bread (8 oz.),
 cut in halves
 lengthwise
8 oz. cream cheese
1 (1 oz.) env. Hidden
 Valley Ranch
 milk salad dressing
 mix
4 c. shredded cheese

Slice bread crosswise into 1 inch fingers, leaving attached. Mix cream cheese and salad dressing together; spread on bread. Pile on toppings. Broil until brown and bubbly.

SAUSAGE AND CHEESE BALLS

1 lb. sausage
1 pkg. Cracker Barrel
  sharp Cheddar
  cheese, shredded
3 c. Bisquick

Combine all ingredients. Shape into bite-size balls. Bake 10 to 15 minutes, until browned at 350°.

Tip: Freeze them on cookie sheets and after the individual balls are frozen, put the entire batch in a freezer bag and keep frozen. This way you have quick hors d'oeuvres anytime needed. You can use whatever amount of balls needed for the occasion. If baking frozen balls, baking time will be slightly longer.

MEXICAN ROLL-UPS

8 oz. cream cheese
4 green onions,
  chopped fine
8 oz. sour cream
1 can green chilies,
  chopped
Garlic salt to taste

Mix all ingredients. Spread on flour tortillas and roll. Refrigerate for 2 to 3 hours. Slice into bite-size pieces. Serve with taco sauce or picante sauce for dip.

CHEESY CHERRY TOMATOES

Hors d'oeuvres.

½ lb. Bleu cheese
½ c. sour cream
1 tsp. minced onion
Dash of pepper
1 basket cherry
  tomatoes

Mash cheese and blend in sour cream, onion, and pepper. Cut a slice from tops of tomatoes and scoop out centers. Fill tomato shells with cheese mixture.

APPLE DIP

1 (8 oz.) pkg. cream
  cheese,
  softened
1 c. strawberry jam
1 (8 oz.) container
  whipped
  topping

Whip cream cheese; add jam and blend well. Gently fold in topping until evenly blended. Dip apple into mixture.

Apples may be dipped in lemon juice before serving to preserve.

VEGETABLE DIP

1 c. cottage cheese
1 c. mayonnaise
1 pkg. Hidden Valley
  salad dressing
  mix

Mix together and chill.

ARTICHOKE DIP

2 cans artichokes,
  chopped and
  drained well
2 c. mayonnaise
2 c. Parmesan
  cheese, grated

Mix all ingredients. Bake in pie pan. Bake in oven at 350° for 30 minutes or until brown. Serve with crackers.

RANCH SAUCE

1 c. (10½ oz.) tomato
  soup
1 Tbsp. brown sugar
¼ c. pickle relish

Boil this all together; makes 1½ cups.

Use on hamburgers or hot dogs.

FRUIT DIP

1 jar marshmallow
  creme
1 (8 oz.) cream
  cheese

Mix marshmallow creme and cream cheese well. Use any kind of fruit for dipping.

STUFFED MUSHROOMS

1 pkg. bacon
1 (8 oz.) pkg. cream
  cheese
1 lb. fresh
  mushrooms

Fry bacon until crispy. Wash mushrooms and pull off the stems; save for use in another dish. Let cream cheese soften to room temperature. Crumble bacon onto softened cream cheese and mix in 2 tablespoons of the bacon drippings. Pile mixture in the button cavity of the mushroom. Place on cookie sheet and broil 2 to 3 minutes. Serve as a warm hors d'oeuvre.

CHILI-CHEESE DIP

1½ lb. Velveeta
   cheese
1 can Ro-Tel
   tomatoes
1 medium can chili
   (without beans)

Melt cheese, then add chili and tomatoes. Mix together well. Serve in a chafing dish.

QUICK TUNA DIP

1 pt. sour cream
2 Tbsp. prepared
   mustard
½ c. chili sauce or
   catsup
1 env. onion soup mix
7 oz. can tuna

Blend together sour cream, prepared mustard, and catsup. Stir in onion soup mix and tuna; mix well. Chill until ready to serve. Serve with cucumber wedges, chips, cherry tomatoes, corn chips, and celery pieces.

MUNCHIN CRACKERS

1 box oyster crackers
1 c. salad oil (Wesson
   preferred)
1 pkg. salad dressing
   (Hidden Valley
   Ranch)
1 tsp. dill seed

Mix oil, dressing, and dill seed. Put crackers in a bowl that has a cover. Pour the dressing over; shake or stir 3 or 4 times. Cover and let stand overnight. Don't refrigerate. Keep at room temperature.

STRAWBERRY LEMONADE

1 qt. strawberries,
   sliced
3 c. cold water
¾ c. lemon juice
¾ c. sugar
2 c. club soda

In blender, puree strawberries. In 2 quart pitcher, combine pureed strawberries, water, lemon juice, and sugar. Stir well. Add club soda before serving.

Frozen strawberries may be used. Finished drink without club soda may be frozen.

RED SATIN PARTY PUNCH

1 pt. apple juice
1 qt. cranberry juice
10 (7 oz.) bottles 7-Up

Combine liquids.

This is so simple, yet so tasty and colorful. Looks so beautiful in the punch bowl. Be sure to make ice out of 7-Up and not out of water.

ROSY TEA QUENCHER

⅓ c. Lipton
  decaffeinated
  lemon flavored iced
  tea mix with
  NutraSweet
3½ c. cranberry juice
  cocktail
3 c. water
1 c. unsweetened
  pineapple juice

In large pitcher, combine all ingredients. Serve with ice and garnish, if desired, with lemon slices.

APPLE-HONEY TEA

1 (12 oz.) can frozen
  apple cider
2 Tbsp. instant tea
  powder
1 Tbsp. honey
½ tsp. cinnamon

In medium saucepan, reconstitute apple cider concentrate according to package directions. Add instant tea powder, honey, and cinnamon. Stir to blend; heat through.

RUSSIAN TEA

2 c. Tang
1 c. Lipton instant tea
  with lemon
½ c. sugar (optional)
½ tsp. cloves
1 tsp. cinnamon

Mix all ingredients and store in glass jar. Use approximately 1 heaping teaspoonful per cup. Add hot water just like instant coffee.

TROPICAL PUNCH

1 (46 oz.) can
  Hawaiian
  Punch fruit juicy
  red
1 (6 oz.) can orange
  juice concentrate
  (undiluted)
1 (6 oz.) can
  lemonade or
  limeade
  concentrate
  (undiluted)

Mix ingredients; chill for 2 hours. Pour punch over block of ice in punch bowl. Float strawberries and thin slices of oranges, lemons, and limes on top.

LEMON JULIUS

1 (6 oz.) can frozen
  lemonade
  concentrate
1 (6 oz.) can frozen
  orange juice
  concentrate
4 c. water
2 c. vanilla ice cream

Combine ingredients in blender; blend on medium speed until mixed and foamy. If blender is too small to hold all the ingredients, make half the recipe at a time and combine the 2 mixes.

PEACH PUNCH

1 large peach Jell-O
2 c. boiling water
2 c. cold water
1 can peach Hi-C
1 large Mountain
  Dew

Mix, then serve over ice.

STRAWBERRY TEA

6 c. water
1 c. sugar
½ c. pure lemon juice
¼ c. instant tea
1 pkg. sweetened
  strawberries

Mix strawberries and sugar in a bowl and let stand 10 to 15 minutes. Mix water, tea, and lemon juice, then stir in strawberries. Add sugar to taste. Chill; serve over ice.

MOCK CHAMPAGNE

**46 oz. can pineapple
  juice
46 oz. can apple juice
12 oz. can frozen
  lemonade
  concentrate
3 qt. ginger ale
½ c. sugar**

Combine pineapple juice, apple juice, lemonade concentrate, and sugar. Stir well until sugar dissolves. Store in freezer overnight or longer.

When ready to serve, remove from freezer 3 to 4 hours before using so juice becomes mushy. Break up and place in large punch bowl and add ginger ale. Do not add ice. The slushy juice keeps punch cold.

LIME PUNCH

**2 pkg. lemon-lime
  Kool-Aid
2 qt. water
40 oz. unsweetened
  pineapple juice
2 c. sugar
Ginger ale**

Freeze first 4 ingredients 5 hours ahead of time. Take out of freezer. Add ¾ part ginger ale.

HOT APPLE CIDER

**1 qt. apple juice
¼ c. sugar
¼ c. "red hots"
  cinnamon
  candy**

Mix all ingredients over medium heat, stirring until sugar and candy are dissolved. Bring to a boil. Simmer for 20 minutes.

MOCHA COFFEE

**½ c. instant coffee
  granules
½ c. sugar
1 c. dry milk or coffee
  creamer
2 Tbsp. cocoa**

Blend in blender or food processor. Store in tightly closed jar.

To use, combine 2 rounded teaspoons of mixture in 1 cup boiling water. Stir well.

SOUPS, SALADS, VEGETABLES

BROCCOLI SOUP

1 (10 oz.) pkg. frozen
chopped
broccoli (can use
fresh)
1 (10¾ oz.) can
cream of
mushroom soup
(undiluted)
1½ c. milk
2 Tbsp. margarine
1 c. shredded
Cheddar
cheese

Cook broccoli in large saucepan according to package directions (omit salt). Drain well. Stir in remaining ingredients until thoroughly heated. Serve immediately.

FRENCH ONION SOUP

18 c. water or broth
25 beef bouillon
cubes
Lots of onions in lots
of butter
Provolone cheese

Cook water and bouillon cubes together. Saute onions in butter; add to water. Simmer. Add Provolone cheese on top of soup in bowl. Cook for 1½ hours.

CHEESE SOUP

Large brick Velveeta
cheese
1 c. milk
1 c. diced ham
2 finely chopped
green onion stalks

Slice cheese; place in microwave bowl. Put ½ of the milk in the bowl. Put it in the microwave; check it every 2 minutes. When the cheese starts to melt, take it out and stir and add a little milk. Put back in the microwave; let finish melting. Take it out; add the rest of the milk, ham, and onions. Put back in the microwave for 2 minutes. Take it out, stir, and serve fast.

BEAN SOUP

1½ c. soup beans
1 thick slice ham,
  diced
1 carrot, shredded
1 celery stalk, diced
1 small potato, diced

Cover beans with water (a quart or more); boil slow (tilt lid of pot) 2 to 2½ hours, until beans are soft and ham cooked. Add salt and pepper to taste. Add carrot, celery, and potato. Simmer until soft.

CREAM OF MUSHROOM SOUP

1 c. canned
  mushrooms
2 c. thin white sauce
1 Tbsp. minced onion
Salt and pepper
Paprika

Chop mushrooms. Add white sauce, mushroom liquor, and onion. Cook over hot water, stirring constantly, for 10 minutes. Rub through sieve. Reheat. Season to taste. Garnish with paprika.

CRABMEAT BISQUE

2 cans condensed
  tomato soup
1 can condensed split
  pea soup
  without ham
1 c. milk
2 cans crabmeat
⅓ c. cooking sherry

Simmer soups with milk. Stir in cooking sherry and add drained crabmeat. Heat and serve. Delicious served with toasted English muffins.

HAMBURGER SOUP

1 lb. hamburger,
  browned
1 can water or 2
  cubes beef bouillon,
  diluted
1 can beef bouillon
Tomato juice
Vegetables (any
  combination
  you desire)

Cook until vegetables are done or use frozen vegetables mixed.

QUICK CREAMY VEGETABLE SOUP

1½ c. water
½ tsp. salt
1 c. mixed vegetables
(frozen)
¼ c. celery, chopped
1 (16 oz.) can cream
of chicken soup

Bring water and salt to boil. Add vegetables and celery and cook 10 minutes. Blend in the soup. Reduce flame to simmer and heat 2 to 3 minutes longer.

TOMATO SOUP

1 qt. tomato juice or
1 large can
whole tomatoes
½ tsp. sugar
½ c. raw macaroni
3 Tbsp. oleo
Black pepper or hot
green peppers

Combine ingredients and cook.

IRISH POTATO SOUP

4 medium potatoes,
peeled and
diced
1 stalk celery, cut fine
1 small onion, cut fine

Cook all together until potatoes are tender. Pour off water. Add milk to cover and 1 stick of oleo. Salt and pepper to taste.

CHICKEN PASTA SALAD

1 box twisted noodles
1 c. cooked chicken
breast, diced
½ c. diced celery
½ c. diced carrots
8 oz. shredded
Cheddar cheese

Saute carrots and celery in tablespoon of margarine approximately 20 minutes. Cook noodles as package directs. Mix into carrots and celery; saute for an additional 10 minutes. Combine in large casserole dish noodles, chicken mixture, and Cheddar cheese. Bake at 350° until cheese melts. Allow 15 minutes in oven or 5 minutes in microwave.

CHICKEN AND GRAPE SALAD

1 lb. cooked chicken, diced
1 c. celery, chopped
1 c. mayonnaise
2 c. seedless grapes
2 green onions, chopped fine

Mix all ingredients together and serve on a bed of lettuce. Garnish with green olives and hard-boiled egg slices.

GOURMET TURKEY SALAD

3 c. turkey, cubed (preferably the breast)
¾ c. celery, chopped
¾ c. broken pecan halves

Mix all ingredients together with about ½ cup of mayonnaise or until medium consistency. Add gourmet grind black pepper and chill until served. Serve on lettuce covered salad plates, garnished with wedges of tomato or pineapple slices. Serve with hot poppy seed rolls.

FRESH SPINACH SALAD

1 lb. fresh spinach
4 hard cooked eggs, chopped
8 slices bacon, fried and crumbled
¼ c. chopped green onions
½ c. Italian salad dressing

Remove large veins from spinach; tear into small pieces. Combine spinach, eggs, and bacon. Add onions; toss lightly. Add dressing just before serving.

CRANBERRY-APPLE SALAD

1 (3 oz.) pkg. strawberry Jell-O
1¼ c. boiling water
1 can cranberry sauce
2 c. chopped apples
Nuts

Dissolve Jell-O in boiling water. Break up cranberry sauce with fork; add to Jell-O. Chill until thick. Add apples and nuts. Chill.

CAULIFLOWER SALAD

1 medium head
  cauliflower
1 can cut green
  beans, drained
1 env. onion salad
  dressing mix
⅔ c. salad oil
⅓ c. vinegar

Separate cauliflower and cook in salted water until tender (10 minutes). Drain. Put cauliflower and beans in a bowl. Put dressing mix, oil, and vinegar in a screw jar with lid. Shake well and put in vegetables. Chill overnight. Shake occasionally and serve on lettuce.

PEA AND BACON SALAD

1 pkg. frozen peas
8 slices bacon, fried
  and crumbled
  or broken into
  small pieces
1 c. sour cream
Pinch of salt

Thaw peas. Drain bacon on paper towel. Combine all ingredients.

CARROT SALAD

3 large carrots
1 c. raisins
4 Tbsp. salad
  dressing
1 can crushed
  pineapple,
  drained
⅓ to ½ c. sugar

Mix sugar and salad dressing together. Fold in carrot, pineapple, and raisins.

RHUBARB SALAD

4 c. rhubarb, diced
1½ c. water
2 c. sugar
½ tsp. salt
1 small can crushed
  pineapple

Boil rhubarb, water, sugar, and salt together; add pineapple. Put in a 9x13 inch pan or jello mold.

ENGLISH PEA SALAD

1 (16 oz.) can English
  peas, drained
1 (2 oz.) jar pimentos,
  dried
2 medium Delicious
  apples, diced
1 lb. American
  cheese, cubed
¼ c. mayonnaise

Peel, core, and dice apples, coating with a little of the mayonnaise. Cut cheese. Place all ingredients in bowl. Mix well with mayonnaise.

ORANGE SALAD

1 c. small curd
  cottage cheese
1 c. Cool Whip
1 small can mandarin
  oranges
½ pkg. orange Jell-O
  (dry) or 3 Tbsp.

Drain oranges well. Mix together cottage cheese, Cool Whip, and dry orange Jell-O. Add drained oranges. Stir with fork gently but thoroughly. Serve chilled.

PEAR SALAD

1 large can pears
1 (8 oz.) pkg. cream
  cheese
1 (3 oz.) pkg. black
  raspberry jello
¾ c. chopped pecans
1 small ctn. Cool
  Whip

Drain juice from pears and boil. Mix with jello and set aside to cool. Mash pears; add cream cheese and mix well. Add to cool jello and add pecans. Fold in Cool Whip and pour in 8x8 inch glass dish; chill.

COCONUT SALAD

2 cans mandarin
  oranges
1 large can crushed
  pineapple,
  drained
2 c. coconut
2 c. miniature
  marshmallows
2 c. sour cream

Mix and refrigerate overnight.

FIVE CUP SALAD

1 c. mandarin
   oranges,
   drained
1 c. miniature
   marshmallows
1 c. flaked coconut
1 c. crushed
   pineapple
1 c. sour cream

Break orange slices in halves. Add pineapple and rest of ingredients. Mix; chill before serving.

APRICOT AND SOUR CREAM SALAD

1 small pkg. lemon
   jello
1 c. apricot nectar
½ c. hot water
1 (8 oz.) ctn. sour
   cream
1 can mandarin
   oranges

Make jello with nectar and hot water (use juice from oranges and water to measure ½ cup). Cool. Add sour cream and oranges. Refrigerate and serve.

MINT MIST SALAD

1 (20 oz.) can crushed
   pineapple
1 pkg. unflavored
   gelatin
⅓ c. mint flavored
   apple jelly
1 c. whipped cream

Drain pineapple; reserve juice. Soften gelatin in ½ cup pineapple juice. Place over low heat, stirring constantly, until gelatin dissolves. Remove from heat. Add jelly. Stir until melted. Add pineapple and remainder of juice. Chill until thick and syrupy. Fold cream into gelatin mixture. Turn into a lightly oiled 4 cup mold. Chill until set.

BEET SALAD

1 can sliced beets
1 can crushed
   pineapple
1 pkg. raspberry jello

Dissolve jello in ½ the water (boiling) as the package calls for, ½ cup for small, 1 cup for large. When cooled, add canned beets and pineapple, juice and all.

One teaspoon of vinegar will enhance flavor and help it set.

PINK FLUFF SALAD

1 (No. 2) can crushed
   pineapple
   (including juice)
1 large pkg. Cool
   Whip
1 large pkg.
   raspberry jello
1 small ctn. small
   curd cottage cheese

Heat pineapple to boiling. Add jello to dissolve. Let cool to room temperature. Add cottage cheese and Cool Whip. Refrigerate.

SOUTH OF THE BORDER RICE

1 c. rice
2 cans cream of
   chicken soup
8 oz. sour cream
2 or 3 cans (4 oz.)
   green chilies
10 oz. Cheddar
   cheese, grated

Cook rice. When dry and fluffy, add soup, sour cream, and juice from chilies. Place ⅓ of mixture in large flat greased pan. Add layer of chilies and a layer of cheese. Repeat twice. Bake with cheese on top in 350° oven for 30 to 40 minutes.

FRIED RICE

Precooked rice
Bacon, cooked and
   crumbled
Scallions, chopped
   and cooked in bacon
   grease
2 eggs, scrambled in
   butter
Soy sauce

Put all ingredients, except soy sauce, in large frying pan. Crush bacon into bits. Pour in some soy sauce and heat through.

BAKED RICE

1 c. Minute rice
1 stick butter
1 can beef broth or
   consomme
1 (4 oz.) can sliced
   mushrooms, drained

Mix all the ingredients and bake at 300° in a covered casserole for 1 hour.

BROWN BUTTER RICE

3 c. chicken broth
Juice of 1 lemon
1 c. white long grain
    rice
¼ c. butter

Bring chicken broth and lemon juice to a boil in a medium size saucepan. Add rice; return to a boil, then reduce heat. Cover and simmer until liquid is absorbed, about 20 minutes, over medium heat. Melt and simmer butter until it becomes richly browned. Stir into cooked rice.

HOLIDAY HOMINY

2 cans hominy
1 (8 oz.) sour cream
1 (10 oz.) Monterey
    Jack cheese
    with jalapeno
1 c. grated Cheddar
    cheese
⅓ c. oleo or butter

Cook hominy until dry. Cut up cheese in Pyrex dish and pour hominy over. Add salt, pepper, and sour cream. Spread cheese and dot with butter. Bake at 350° until bubbly.

BAKED ONIONS IN CASSEROLE

Large Bermuda
    onions
Butter
Pepper
Little salt

Peel large, uniform onions and slice about ½ inch thick. Place in a buttered casserole, making about 3 layers and on each layer put plenty of butter and pepper - not much salt and no water. Cover and cook in a slow oven (300° to 325°) until done. Take cover off and brown, if they have not already browned.

SPINACH-ARTICHOKE CASSEROLE

2 pkg. frozen
    chopped
    spinach
1 can artichoke
    hearts
1 (8 oz.) cream
    cheese
1 onion
Oil or margarine

Cook spinach. Season, butter, and set aside. Saute onion in margarine. Soften cream cheese with fork in onion while warm. Mix all in casserole. Bake at 300° until warm.

EGGPLANT PARMIGIANA

1 large (about 2 lb.)
   eggplant
¾ c. olive oil
1½ c. canned tomato
   sauce
¼ c. grated
   Parmesan
   cheese
½ lb. Mozzarella
   cheese, sliced
   thin

Peel eggplant and cut into ¼ inch slices. Fry on both sides in olive oil in skillet until browned. Drain well on paper towels. Put layer of eggplant into bottom of shallow baking dish; cover with some tomato sauce, a little Parmesan cheese, and few slices of Mozzarella. Repeat these layers until all ingredients are used and ending with the layer of Mozzarella. Bake, uncovered, in 400°F. oven for 15 minutes.

ASPARAGUS DIJON

3 cans vertical pack
   asparagus
1½ c. mayonnaise
3 Tbsp. lemon juice
¼ c. Dijon mustard
1 c. heavy cream,
   whipped

Mix mayonnaise, lemon juice, and mustard, then fold in whipped cream. Drain asparagus and heat in baking dish, then put sauce on top and put under broiler until lightly browned. *It browns very quickly.*

ITALIAN ZUCCHINI

1 or 2 zucchini
   (unpeeled),
   sliced ¼ inch thick
½ c. Italian dressing
½ lb. fresh whole
   mushrooms
⅓ c. grated
   Parmesan
   cheese

Quickly saute zucchini in dressing over medium to high heat for 5 to 7 minutes, adding mushrooms the last 2 minutes. Zucchini should be slightly crisp. Pour into serving dish and sprinkle with Parmesan cheese.

BROCCOLI AND LINGUINI

½ lb. bacon, cut into
  pieces
1 bunch broccoli, cut
  into flowerets
1 lb. linguini

Cook broccoli in boiling water on the hard side. Drain; reserve liquid. Cook bacon in skillet until crisp; remove. In bacon drippings, brown garlic; flavor with dash of hot pepper flakes. Add broccoli and saute until flavored with bacon mixture. Add ½ cup of reserved liquid.

Separately boil linguini to taste. Toss with broccoli mixture and serve. Add remaining liquid to provide broth. Season with Parmesan cheese.

LEMON-BUTTERED BROCCOLI

1 (10 oz.) pkg. frozen
  broccoli spears
¼ c. hot melted
  butter
1 Tbsp. lemon juice

1. In 1 quart saucepan, cook broccoli following directions for cooking on package. Place in serving bowl.
2. Combine butter and lemon juice. Pour over broccoli. Garnish with lemon slices.

CAULIFLOWER-BROCCOLI DISH

1 head cauliflower,
  cooked whole
12 pieces broccoli,
  cooked
¼ c. melted butter
Paprika

Place cooked cauliflower in center of round serving plate. Surround with broccoli. Pour melted butter over top. Sprinkle lightly with paprika.

CAULIFLOWER WITH CHEESE AND BROWNED BUTTER

1 medium-size head
  cauliflower
Salt and freshly
  ground pepper
6 Tbsp. butter
½ c. freshly grated
  Parmesan or
  Romano cheese

Cut off the outer leaves, then core the cauliflower, leaving the head intact. Boil this in a large pot with about an inch of salted water. (The best way is to steam it, covered, on a rack over water. Steaming takes 10 to 12 minutes, depending on size, and boiling will take 1 or 2 minutes longer.) Cook just until a sharp knife can penetrate the stems. Sprinkle with salt and pepper to taste. Keep warm.

Melt butter in a small saucepan set over medium heat, shaking the pan now and again until the foam dies down and the butter is a light nut brown. Sprinkle cheese over the cauliflower, then pour the sizzling butter over the top. This can be served immediately, or if you must, let it sit at room temperature and reheat in a moderate oven.

BEST EVER BROCCOLI CASSEROLE

2 boxes frozen
  broccoli,
  chopped
8 oz. Velveeta cheese
  (no
  substitutions)
1½ sticks butter or
  margarine
28 Ritz crackers (no
  substitutions)

Cook 2 boxes of frozen chopped broccoli as directed on box. Drain well and set aside. Crush Ritz crackers and set aside.

In saucepan or double boiler, melt 1 stick margarine or butter and Velveeta cheese. Add cheese sauce to cooked broccoli. Put ½ of the cheese and broccoli in a greased casserole dish. Add ½ of the cracker crumbs. Put in remaining broccoli-cheese mixture and top with the remaining crackers. Bake at 350° for 30 minutes.

May be prepared the day before and refrigerated.

CABBAGE SURPRISE

1 (10 oz.) can
  condensed
  cream of celery
  soup
1 c. sour cream
1 tsp. caraway seed
1 medium head
  cabbage, cut
  into wedges

In a large skillet, blend soup, sour cream, and caraway seeds; add the cabbage. Cover and cook over low heat until the cabbage is tender. Cook for about 20 minutes.

ZUCCHINI CASSEROLE

2 lb. zucchini, sliced
8 oz. cream cheese
Salt and pepper to
  taste
Bread crumbs,
  buttered

Boil zucchini until tender. Beat cheese and zucchini together until fluffy. Add salt and pepper to taste. Put in casserole and top with bread crumbs. Bake at 325° until heated through.

CORN CASSEROLE

1 can whole kernel
  corn
  (undrained)
1 can cream style
  corn
1 box Jiffy corn bread
  mix
1 c. sour cream
1 stick oleo

Mix ingredients together and pour into baking dish and bake for 1 hour at 350°.

Optional: The last 10 minutes, take out and put grated Cheddar cheese on top.

COUNTRY CREAMED STYLE CORN

2½ lb. box frozen
  corn
1 tsp. salt
3 tsp. sugar
¾ c. whipping cream
  or coffee cream
2 to 3 tsp. cornstarch

Cook corn in a small amount of water. Add salt, sugar, and cream. Bring to boil and thicken with mixture of cornstarch and a little cream.

GREEN BEAN CATALINA

2 large cans whole
   green beans
1 lb. bacon
1 bottle Catalina
   dressing

Bundle 5 green beans and secure with bacon. Place all bundles in a baking dish. Cover with Catalina dressing and bake at 340° for 30 minutes.

GREEN BEAN CASSEROLE

1 can green beans
1 can French fried
   onions
1 can condensed
   cream of
   mushroom soup

Drain beans; combine with soup and ½ can onions. Pour into greased 1 quart casserole. Bake at 350° for 20 minutes. Garnish with remaining onions and return to oven for about 3 minutes.

MINTED CARROTS

1 pkg. carrots, cut in
   strips
¼ c. butter
3 Tbsp. honey
2 tsp. fresh mint
   leaves or
   parsley

Cook carrots in boiling water (salted) for about 15 minutes. Drain. Combine butter, honey, and mint. Heat to melt butter. Add carrots and heat over low heat, stirring occasionally until well glazed.

HONEY GLAZED CARROTS

6 large carrots,
   peeled
Salt
¼ c. honey
1 c. (4 oz.) grated
   Cheddar
   cheese

Cut carrots in halves crosswise. Cook in boiling salted water until just tender, about 15 minutes; drain. Roll each carrot in honey. Place in 1 quart greased baking dish; sprinkle with grated cheese. Bake at 350° for 5 to 10 minutes or until cheese is melted.

For added color, sprinkle with finely chopped parsley.

HERBED POTATOES

½ c. melted oleo
1 env. onion soup mix
1 Tbsp. rosemary
3 to 4 peeled
    potatoes

Combine oleo, soup mix, and rosemary. Scrub potatoes and cut into ½ inch slices. Coat potatoes with mixture. Arrange in greased casserole. Cover and bake at 350°F. for 45 minutes.

CRISPY POTATO BALLS

Mashed potatoes
1 egg
2 Tbsp. water
Crushed corn flakes
    or your favorite
    unsweetened dry
    cereal

Prepare mashed potatoes as usual with a little onion salt. Beat egg; dilute with water. Roll potatoes into balls. Dip balls into egg mixture, then into crushed cereal. Place onto greased baking sheet and bake at 375° until well heated (for 20 minutes). Serve immediately.

SEASONED POTATOES

4 to 6 potatoes
1 stick oleo, melted
1 pkg. Original
    Hidden Valley
    salad dressing mix

Wash potatoes; do not peel. Slice crossways and layer in casserole. Pour melted butter over the potatoes and sprinkle with Hidden Valley mix. Bake at 350° for 1 hour.

SWISS AU GRATIN POTATOES

2 lb. (about 5 c.)
    potatoes,
    peeled and thinly
    sliced
Salt and pepper
¼ c. butter, cut into
    small pieces
1 c. (4 oz.) grated
    Swiss cheese
1½ c. whipping
    cream

Place half of the potato slices in greased 2 quart shallow baking dish. Sprinkle with salt and pepper and half of the butter and cheese. Repeat layers, ending with the cheese. Pour cream over top. Cover with foil. Bake at 325° for 1 hour and 15 minutes. Remove foil and bake 30 to 45 minutes or until top is lightly browned and potatoes are tender.

COUNTRY FRIED POTATOES

4 or 5 potatoes,
   sliced
½ c. shortening or oil
1 c. sliced onions
2 tsp. salt
¼ tsp. black pepper

Heat shortening or oil in heavy skillet over low heat. Arrange a layer of sliced potatoes and sliced onion; repeat. Sprinkle with salt and pepper. Cover tightly. Cook over low heat for 15 minutes. Uncover and increase heat slightly and saute for 10 minutes longer or until potatoes are crisp and brown on underside. Do not stir. Fold in half as with an omelet. Serve on a hot platter.

CANDIED SWEET POTATOES

Canned sweet
   potatoes,
   drained
Butter
Brown sugar
Large marshmallows

Place desired number of sweet potatoes in shallow baking dish. Top generously with slices of butter. Sprinkle generously with brown sugar. Bake at 350° for 1 hour. Remove from oven. Top with marshmallows spaced 2 inches apart. Return to oven; bake until marshmallows are puffy and lightly browned (watch carefully).

SQUASH WITH ONIONS

2 lb. yellow summer
   squash
3 medium onions,
   sliced thin
3 Tbsp. butter or oleo
½ tsp. salt
¼ tsp. pepper

Wash squash and dice. Combine all ingredients in large skillet. Cover and cook for 20 to 30 minutes, until tender. Stir frequently.

STEAMED SNOW PEAS

⅓ lb. snow peas
1 Tbsp. butter
Nutmeg
Salt and pepper

Bring 6 cups water to a boil in a medium saucepan over medium heat. Set snow peas in steamer or strainer above water and steam for 1 minute. Drain well. Heat butter in a medium skillet over medium high heat. Add snow peas and saute until tender, about 1 to 2 minutes. Season with nutmeg and salt and pepper to taste. Serve at once.

BAKED BEANS

1 large can pork and
  beans
1 tsp. mustard
¼ c. brown sugar
1 small can crushed
  pineapple
Strip of bacon

Bake at 350° for 1 to 1½ hours.

EASY BEANS

2 cans chilli beans
½ green pepper,
  diced
6 to 8 oz. Mozzarella
  cheese

Use microwave-safe casserole dish. Empty in chilli beans. Add green pepper. Stir in grated Mozzarella cheese. Cook on HIGH in microwave for 8 to 10 minutes, until cheese melts (or 350° for ½ hour).

This is an easy recipe to use when bar-b-queing. Also great to cook in the microwave in the summer to keep the house cool.

MAIN DISHES

BEEF TIPS WITH PEPPERS

1½ to 2 lb. sirloin
2 large, thinly sliced
  onions
2 large, thinly sliced
  green pepper
A.1. Sauce
Worcestershire sauce

Cut sirloin into thin strips. In a large skillet, quickly brown steak, adding A.1. Sauce and Worcestershire sauce to taste. Add peppers and onions. Cook until tender, about 10 to 15 minutes. Serve alone or over rice.

CHICKEN FRIED STEAK

1½ lb. round steak
1 egg, beaten and
  blended with 1
  Tbsp. milk
1 c. cracker crumbs,
  finely crushed
¼ c. salad oil

Pound steak. Cut into serving pieces. Dip into egg mixture, then in crumbs. Brown meat slowly in hot oil. Cover; cook 45 to 60 minutes over low heat.

RANCH STYLE RUMP ROAST

5 lb. rump roast
1 tsp. salt
½ tsp. paprika
1 small onion
½ tsp. pepper

Mix salt, pepper, and paprika; sprinkle evenly over meat. Chop onion fine. Place meat in roasting pan, fat side up. Spread onion over the top of meat. Cook at 300° for 2 hours for medium well done or 1 hour and 40 minutes for rare or 2½ hours for very well done. Cook potatoes with roast until nicely browned, about 1½ hours. Prepare gravy with stock in roaster by adding 2 cups of water; heat to boiling point. Stir in 2 tablespoons of flour mixed with 2 tablespoons of cold water. Cook until thickened.

GRILLED FLANK STEAK

4 (¼ to 1½ lb.) flank
  steaks
Garlic powder
1 c. soy sauce
½ c. Worcestershire
  sauce
½ c. vegetable oil

Sprinkle flank steak lightly on both sides with garlic powder. Prick both sides of steak with fork and place in large, shallow pan. Combine remaining ingredients; pour over steak. Cover and marinate steak 8 hours or overnight in refrigerator, turning occasionally. Remove steak from marinade. Grill over medium coals 7 to 9 minutes on each side for medium rare.

BARBECUED BRISKET

1 (3½ to 4 lb.) beef
  brisket
¼ c. plus 2 Tbsp.
  liquid smoke
1 tsp. salt
1 Tbsp. garlic powder
1 Tbsp. onion
  powder

Line a 13x9x2 inch pan with heavy-duty aluminum foil. Place brisket in pan; sprinkle with liquid smoke and salt. Bring sides of foil up and seal completely. Chill 8 hours. Unwrap and sprinkle with onion and garlic powders. Rewrap and bake at 300° for 4 hours. Serve with your favorite barbeque sauce.

NO PEEK STEW

2 lb. boneless stew,
  well trimmed
1 pkg. dry onion soup
1 can mushroom
  soup
1 can tomato soup
1 can peas and juice

Place all ingredients in casserole with tight fitting lid. Bake at 350° for 3 hours. Serve over rice. Do not peek while baking. Season to taste.

CHEESE ENCHILADAS

1 doz. corn tortillas
8 oz. Velveeta cheese
1 onion, finely
  chopped
8 oz. Monterey Jack
  cheese
1 large can chili

Cube either or both cheeses; use 16 ounces if using only one kind. Mix cheese and onion together. Dip tortilla into hot water and sprinkle with cheese and onion. Roll and place in greased dish. Top with chili and top with cheese and onions. Bake 20 minutes in a 350° oven.

LAZY DAY BEEF PIE

Flour
Salt and pepper
1½ lb. stew meat, cut
    into small
    pieces
½ onion, chopped
2 c. canned mixed
    peas and
    carrots
1 pkg. corn bread mix

Flour and season beef. Slowly cook meat and onion in water for 1½ to 2 hours. Add peas and carrots. Transfer to baking dish. Top with corn bread mix prepared according to package directions. Bake at 425° for 20 minutes.

STROGANOFF

1 lb. hamburger
Chopped onion to
    taste
1 can cream of
    mushroom soup
1 pt. sour cream

Form hamburger into meatballs and pan fry. Saute onions in a little butter. Add remaining ingredients. Blend and serve over rice or noodles.

MOCK STEAK

1 lb. lean hamburger
½ env. dry onion
    soup mix
1 Tbsp.
    Worcestershire
    sauce
1 c. Pepperidge Farm
    stuffing mix
¾ c. tomato juice

Mix and shape into 5 to 6 oblong patties. Charcoal as hamburgers, about 10 minutes.

FLORIDA STEAK

3 lb. ground beef
1 c. instant oats
1 onion, chopped
    real fine
Salt and pepper to
    taste
1 large can cream of
    mushroom
    soup

Mix all ingredients together. Pat into greased baking dish to about ¼ inch thick. Freeze until just solid enough to cut. Cut into desired size squares and fry.

APPLESAUCE MEATBALLS

1 c. corn flakes
2 lb. hamburger
½ c. onions, finely
   chopped
½ c. applesauce
2 small cans tomato
   sauce

Mix ingredients, except tomato sauce. Shape into 24 balls. Season with salt and pepper. Place in roasting pan. Pour 2 small cans tomato sauce over meatballs. Bake at 350° for 1 hour. Serve with mashed potatoes or spaghetti.

PORCUPINE MEAT BALLS

2 lb. hamburger
¼ c. diced onions
1 tsp. salt
¼ tsp. pepper
¾ c. Minute rice

Mix the ingredients together. Form into medium size balls, putting into a pan of which 1 can of tomato soup with 1 can of water has been stirred and heated. Bring to a boil; reduce heat and cook for 1½ hours or until tender.

TACO CASSEROLE

1 lb. ground meat
1 pkg. taco mix
1 can tomato sauce
2 c. water
1 pkg. tortilla chips

Brown meat; add taco mix, tomato sauce, and water. Heat until boiling. Line casserole dish with chips. Pour meat mixture over chips. Add chips to the top. Place in oven until very hot.

5 LAYER CASSEROLE

1 lb. raw hamburger
1 can French style
   green beans
1½ c. shredded
   Mozzarella
   cheese
1 can cream of
   mushroom soup
1 box tater tots

Layer in casserole in order given. Bake 1½ hours at 350°.

CORN BREAD CASSEROLE

1 lb. hamburger meat
1 onion
1 can Ranch Style
   beans
1 pkg. grated
   Cheddar
   cheese
1 pkg. corn bread mix

Brown hamburger meat and onion. Season to taste. Drain grease. Spread meat in bottom of casserole dish. Spread beans on top of meat. Cover beans with cheese. Mix corn bread according to directions. Spread corn bread over casserole. Bake until done at 350°. Cut in squares.

EASY MEATLOAF

1 lb. ground beef
½ c. onion, chopped
1 egg
Ketchup
Oatmeal

Break up meat on a plate or in a bowl. Add 1 egg and mix (with hands). Add the ½ cup chopped onion; also mix. Add ketchup, about 2 medium squeezes, and 1 handful of oatmeal. Mix all together. Form into a loaf. If your loaf is too moist, add more oatmeal; if it is too dry, add some more ketchup. Place loaf in an oven baking dish and bake at 325° for 1 hour.

EASY STUFFED PEPPERS

4 medium bell
   peppers
1 (10 oz.) can chili
   without beans
4 Tbsp. water
1 (12 oz.) can
   Mexican corn,
   drained
2 c. crushed Doritos

Cut off stem ends of peppers. Mix chili, chips, and corn into peppers after removing seeds. Place peppers, standing, into casserole dish and add water. Cover and bake at 350° for 1 hour.

GRANDMA'S POT ROAST

1 (2 to 3 lb.) chuck
   roast
1 can cream of
   mushroom soup
1 can cream of celery
   soup
1 pkg. dry onion soup
   mix

Cut roast into 6 to 8 pieces and place in crock pot. Add cream of mushroom, cream of celery, and dry onion soup to roast; mix well. Cook mixture in crock pot for 4 to 6 hours on HIGH or 8 to 10 hours on LOW, or until meat is tender. Serve over rice or mashed potatoes.

MEXICAN MUFFINS

1 lb. lean ground beef
1 (1¼ oz.) pkg. taco
  seasoning mix
½ c. water
5 English muffins,
  split
1 c. (4 oz.) grated
  Cheddar
  cheese

Brown ground beef; drain. Add seasoning mix and water. Simmer 15 minutes or until liquid is absorbed. Place muffins on cookie sheet; top with meat mixture. Sprinkle cheese over top. Bake at 350° for 10 minutes or until heated through. Makes 5 servings.

HAMBURGER MEDLEY

1 lb. hamburger
1 can onion soup
1 (8 oz.) can tomato
  sauce
1½ c. uncooked
  noodles

Mix together in a greased 1½ quart casserole. Cover tightly and bake in 375° oven for 1 hour. Serves 4.

Great for days when you're in a hurry!

HAMBURGER AND POTATO SURPRISE

1 lb. hamburger
Salt and pepper
1 large potato, sliced
1 large onion, sliced

Divide hamburger into 4 parts; shape into thin patties. Place each patty in center of 10 inch square of foil. Sprinkle with salt and pepper. Cover with slices of potato and onion. Wrap foil securely around hamburger. Bake in oven at 375° to 425° for 45 minutes. Makes 4 servings.

CHILI CASSEROLE

1 (14 oz.) can whole
  chilies
½ lb. sharp Cheddar
  cheese,
  shredded
2 c. milk
3 eggs
½ c. flour

Heat oven to 350°. Butter 1½ quart casserole. Cover with pepper strips and cheese (save some for top). Beat eggs, flour, and milk. Pour over cheese and peppers. Season with salt if desired. Top with cheese. Bake at 350° for 45 minutes.

EASY CROCK-POT CHILI

2 cans chili beans
2 (8 oz.) cans tomato
  sauce
2 lb. ground chuck,
  browned and
  drained
2 Tbsp. minced onion
2 to 3 Tbsp. chili
  seasoning

Put all ingredients in crock-pot. Stir. Cover and cook on LOW for 8 to 10 hours. One to two cups of water may be added if desired.

SWISS CHICKEN

8 chicken breasts
  (boneless,
  skinless)
8 slices Swiss cheese
½ (16 oz.) bag
  Pepperidge
  Farm herb stuffing
  mix
1 c. butter, melted
1 can cream of
  mushroom soup

Preheat oven to 350°. Place chicken in a 9x13 inch dish. Cover each breast with a slice of Swiss cheese. Spread cream of mushroom soup over this. Spread stuffing mix around. Pour 1 cup melted butter over everything. Bake for 50 to 60 minutes.

BACONY CHICKEN

2 whole chicken
  breasts, split
6 strips bacon
⅓ c. butter, softened
2 Tbsp.
  Worcestershire
  sauce
2 Tbsp. chives

Cut 2 slashes across each breast half. Press ½ strip of bacon in each slash. Cream butter, Worcestershire sauce, and chives. Brush mixture over breasts. Bake in 375° oven until brown. Brush with pan drippings during cooking.

DIJON CHICKEN

½ c. mayonnaise
2 Tbsp. soy sauce
½ tsp. garlic or 1
  garlic, pressed
4 chicken breasts

Stir all ingredients, but the chicken breasts, together. Marinate for 20 minutes. Grease grill or broiler. Cook chicken for 15 to 20 minutes, turning once. Brush frequently with marinade.

SWEET SOUR CHICKEN

6 chicken breasts
1 (8 oz.) bottle
  Russian dressing
1 (10 to 12 oz.) jar
  apricot preserves
1 env. Lipton onion
  soup mix

Simmer sauce 5 minutes. Pour cooled sauce over chicken; marinate overnight. Bake 2 hours at slow temperature.

CHICKEN BREAST OREGANO

4 chicken breasts or
  other pieces
1 tsp. oregano
Minute rice
1 can chicken and
  rice soup

Lightly oil baking dish. Place desired amount of uncooked Minute rice in dish. Use recipe on box for salt and water. Add oregano (1 teaspoon) to rice. Place chicken pieces on rice. Pour 1 can chicken and rice soup over top of chicken. Sprinkle oregano lightly on top. Bake, uncovered, for 45 minutes or until chicken is done.

BROCCOLI CHEESE CHICKEN

4 whole chicken
  breasts
4 cans Cheddar
  cheese soup
2 boxes broccoli
  spears

Boil chicken breasts; remove skin. Take chicken off bones and place in pan. Defrost broccoli spears or place in water. Place broccoli spears on top of chicken. Spread Cheddar cheese soup on top of chicken. Bake at 350° for 45 minutes to 1 hour.

For smaller portion, cut recipe in half.

CHICKEN CHEESE ROLLS

3 chicken breasts,
  boned and split
8 oz. whipped cream
  cheese and
  chives
1 Tbsp. butter or
  margarine
6 slices bacon

Place chicken between wax paper and pound to ½ inch thickness. Spread 3 tablespoons cheese on chicken. Dot with ½ teaspoon butter. Fold ends over filling. Wrap 1 slice bacon around each roll.

Place, seam side down, in shallow baking pan. Bake on top rack of oven at 400° for 40 minutes. Broil for approximately 5 minutes, until bacon is crisp.

CHICKEN ENCHILADAS

3 to 4 chicken
  breasts, boiled
  and shredded
1 pkg. flour tortillas
  (8 to 12)
1 pt. whipping cream
1 small can chopped
  green chilies
8 oz. shredded
  Monterey Jack cheese

Mix chicken, chilies, and cheese. Wrap in flour tortillas and lay in baking dish. Pour whipping cream over and top with cheese. Cover and bake at 350° until hot, approximately 25 to 30 minutes.

EASY CHICKEN FINGERS

Boneless, skinless
  chicken
Saltine crackers,
  crushed in
  blender
1 egg, beaten
Oil (for frying)

Using mallet, beat chicken pieces on waxed paper to flatten. Cut chicken to desired shapes or cook in large pieces. Dip chicken in a beaten egg, then roll in crushed cracker crumbs. Place in electric skillet at 350° after oil is hot, using just enough oil to cover bottom of skillet. Cook until brown, turning to coat both sides (usually 20 minutes). Place on paper towel to drain. Can serve with or without sauces.

CHICKEN WINGS

1 (5 lb.) pkg. wings
⅔ c. honey
5 Tbsp. soy sauce
4 Tbsp. brown sugar
5 Tbsp. ketchup

Line broiler pan with foil. Add frozen wings. Sprinkle with salt, pepper, and paprika. Combine honey, sauce, sugar, and ketchup. Pour over wings. Bake at 400° for 1 hour and 15 minutes. Baste every 15 minutes.

OVEN FRIED CHICKEN

1 fryer, cut up
1 c. Bisquick
2 tsp. paprika
2 tsp. salt
¾ stick margarine

Melt margarine in Pyrex dish. Shake chicken pieces in sack containing Bisquick, paprika, and salt. Place chicken in Pyrex dish and bake at 400° for 1 hour, maybe less. Do not cover.

ONION-BAKED CHICKEN

2 to 2½ lb. chicken
 pieces
1 env. Lipton onion
 and
 mushroom soup
 mix
½ c. dry bread
 crumbs

Preheat oven to 375°. Moisten chicken with water. Combine soup mix and bread crumbs. Dip chicken and coat well. Place in large shallow pan and drizzle with melted butter. Bake for 45 minutes or until tender.

LEMON BAKED CHICKEN

1 cut up fryer
½ c. melted butter
 (not margarine)
½ c. lemon juice (2
 lemons)
Salt and pepper to
 taste

Sprinkle chicken with salt and pepper. Arrange chicken, skin side up, in a baking pan. Use a 9x13 inch pan. Mix melted butter and lemon juice. Pour over chicken and bake at 375° until done and crispy, about 50 minutes. *Makes chicken very crispy.*

ROCK CORNISH GAME HENS

3 to 6 Rock Cornish
 game hens
1½ c. soy sauce
½ c. lemon juice
1¼ tsp. powdered
 ginger
1½ cloves garlic,
 crushed

Split Rock Cornish game hens in halves. Put into bowl and pour combined ingredients over them. Marinate overnight or 12 to 24 hours. Turn occasionally.

Place halves on broiler rack, skin side down, in a 350°F. oven for 30 minutes. Turn halves over and continue to bake for another 30 minutes. Serve with rice.

GRILLED TURKEY STEAKS

1 lb. turkey breast
 steaks (¾ to 1
 inch thick)
½ c. white grape juice
¼ c. soy sauce
1 Tbsp. vegetable oil
¼ tsp. garlic powder

Combine juice, soy sauce, oil, and garlic in glass dish. Add turkey steaks, turning to coat both sides. Cover and marinate at least 2 hours or up to 24 hours. Turn steaks in marinade several times. Grill drained steaks over medium hot coals 8 to 10 minutes per side, basting with marinade a couple of times. Turkey steaks are done when there is no pink in center of meat.

EASY DOES IT TURKEY QUICHE

2½ to 3 c. stuffing
  (leftover) or 1 (6 oz.)
  box chicken flavor
1 c. chopped, cooked
  turkey
1 c. shredded Swiss
  cheese
4 beaten eggs
1 (5⅓ oz.) can
  evaporated
  milk

If using stuffing mix, prepare as directed on package. Press stuffing into a 9 inch pie plate or quiche pan, forming a crust. Bake in a 400° oven for 10 minutes. Combine meat and cheese.

In another bowl, beat eggs, milk, and ⅛ teaspoon pepper. Sprinkle meat/cheese mixture into pie crust. Pour egg mixture on top. Lower oven temperature to 350°. Bake quiche for 30 to 35 minutes or till center is set. Let stand for 10 minutes before serving. Garnish with a tomato wedge.

TURKEY GOULASH

1 lb. ground turkey
1 c. macaroni
1 can cream of
  mushroom soup
1 (18 oz.) can tomato
  sauce
1 (4 oz.) bag Cheddar
  cheese

Brown turkey. Cook macaroni and drain. Add macaroni, mushroom soup, and tomato sauce to turkey. Mix well. Sprinkle cheese on top and let melt.

BAKED BLUEFISH FILLETS

2 bluefish fillets
2 lemons
Mayonnaise
Bread crumbs
Salt and pepper

Slice lemons very thin. Lay on cookie sheet. Put fillets on top with skin facing lemon slices. Add salt and pepper. Spread generously with Hellmann's mayonnaise and sprinkle bread crumbs on top. Bake for 1 hour in oven at 350°.

DILL SWORDFISH

6 swordfish steaks
1 Tbsp. oil
2 Tbsp. dill weed
¼ c. butter
1 tsp. lemon juice

Brush steaks with oil. Broil the steaks 5 minutes each side for each inch of thickness (over coals is best). Blend together the dill, butter, and lemon juice. Brush onto steaks as they grill and just before serving.

LEMON-BAKED COD

1 lb. cod fillets
1/4 c. margarine or
    butter, melted
2 Tbsp. lemon juice
1/4 c. all-purpose flour
1/2 tsp. salt

Heat oven to 350°. If fish fillets are large, cut into serving pieces. Mix margarine and lemon juice. In another bowl, mix flour and salt. Dip fish into margarine mixture; coat fish with flour mixture. Place fish in ungreased square baking dish, 8x8x2 inches. Pour remaining margarine mixture over fish. Cook, uncovered, until fish flakes easily with fork, 25 to 30 minutes. Garnish with parsley sprigs, paprika, and lemon slices if desired.

CREAMED SALMON

4 slices bacon, fried
    crisp
1 can salmon
    (skinless,
    boneless)
All-purpose flour
Evaporated milk

Fry bacon crisp; drain. Mix approximately 2 tablespoons of flour into the bacon grease; add evaporated milk and 1/4 cup water, mixing constantly. Add salmon; let simmer for about 10 minutes. Serve on plain bread, toast or over rice. Serve with bacon on side if desired.

SALMON PATTIES

1 large can salmon
    (bones
    removed or
    crushed)
5 soda crackers,
    crumbled
2 tsp. corn meal
2 tsp. flour
1 egg

Mix all ingredients by hand; shape into patties. Fry in hot grease. Brown on both sides.

SALMON LOAF

1 can salmon
2/3 c. milk
1 1/2 c. crushed
    cracker crumbs
    or bread crumbs
2 Tbsp. melted butter
Salt and pepper to
    taste

Preheat oven to 400°. Mix all ingredients well. Form into loaf and place in casserole dish. Bake for 1/2 hour or until done.

BAKED ORANGE ROUGHY

4 orange roughy filets
1½ c. sliced
  mushrooms
½ c. grated medium
  Cheddar
  cheese
Salt and pepper

Preheat oven to 450°F. Place filets on individual pieces of heavy-duty foil. Top with raw mushroom slices and cheese. Sprinkle with salt and pepper. Wrap each filet tightly and place on a baking sheet. Bake in oven 10 to 12 minutes.

SHRIMP KABOBS

1 lb. large cooked
  shrimp
1 can chunk
  pineapple
Skewers
Bar-b-que sauce

Alternate shrimp and pineapple onto skewers. Put foil on grill and cook on low just to heat, then baste with bar-b-que sauce. Serve over rice.

BARBEQUED SHRIMP

3 lb. shrimp (20
  count)
1 bottle your favorite
  barbeque sauce
1½ lb. bacon

Peel and devein shrimp, leaving tails on. Butterfly shrimp by slicing along the inner curl. Marinate in sauce 12 to 24 hours. Cut a slice of bacon in half and wrap around each shrimp. Secure with a toothpick. Barbeque individually over hot coals.

BATTER DIPPED FISH

Fish of your choice
  (preferably
  fresh)
1 pkg. pancake mix
Lemon-lime pop
Cooking oil

If fish is frozen, thaw completely. Rinse fish in cold water and pat dry with paper towel. Cut fish into small serving size pieces. Prepare pancake mix, substituting lemon-lime pop for milk. Heat cooking oil in deep-fryer until hot. (A test drop of pancake batter should cook quickly.) Dip fish into batter and deep-fry a few at a time. When batter is lightly browned, remove and place on plate lined with paper towels. Keep warm in oven at 250° until all fish is cooked.

CHIPPER PERCH

1 lb. ocean perch
  fillets
½ c. Caesar salad
  dressing
1 c. crushed potato
  chips
½ c. shredded sharp
  Cheddar
  cheese

Thaw fillets. Dry well. Dip into salad dressing. Place in a single layer on a baking pan, skin side down.

Combine crushed chips and cheese and sprinkle over fillets. Bake (hot) at 500° for 10 to 12 minutes or until fillets flake easily when tested with a fork.

POACHED FISH

1 medium onion,
  sliced
3 slices lemon
1 bay leaf
Black pepper
1 lb. fish fillets

Heat about 1½ inches of water in skillet to boiling. Add lemon, bay leaf, and pepper. Reduce heat to simmer. Add fish. Simmer until flaky, about 5 minutes.

MICROWAVE BAKED FISH

1 (2 oz.) pkg.
  seasoned
  coating mix for fish
1 lb. fish fillets of
  serving size
  pieces of fish
Water

Lightly grease a shallow, 10 inch heat resistant, nonmetallic baking dish. Empty seasoned coating mix into the plastic shaker bag. Moisten fillets with water. Shake off excess water. Arrange fish in greased baking dish. Heat, uncovered, on FULL power for 7 minutes or until fish is easily flaked with a fork.

CRISPY FISH FILLETS

1 c. mayonnaise
1 c. sour cream
1 env. Ranch
  dressing
1 can French fried
  onions, crushed
1½ lb. fish fillets

Mix first 3 ingredients. Dip fish fillets in this, then in crushed onions. Bake at 350° until done.

PORK CHOP AND POTATO CASSEROLE

4 pork chops
2 c. thin sliced
   potatoes
1 onion
1 can mushroom
   soup

Brown pork chops over medium heat. Arrange potatoes in 2 quart dish. Season with salt and pepper. Slice onion very thin and arrange on top of potatoes. Pour ½ can soup over all. Repeat procedure, then place pork chops on top. Cover and bake at 350° for about 1 hour or until tender.

PORK ROAST WITH GARLIC AND ROSEMARY

3 lb. pork roast
2 cloves garlic,
   slivered
1 tsp. rosemary
Salt and pepper

Score fat with a sharp knife. Make small slashes in several places and insert slivers of garlic. Rub surface with rosemary. Sprinkle with salt and pepper. Place roast in a shallow pan. Bake at 375° for about 45 minutes per pound.

SOUTHERN STYLE PORK RIBS

2 to 3 lb. Southern
   (country style)
   pork ribs
1 c. catsup
2 c. water
1 tsp. chile powder
½ tsp. Tabasco sauce

Put the ribs in a small roaster or baking dish. Bake in a 375° oven for 1½ hours. Drain off the accumulated fat. Mix together the catsup, water, chile powder, and Tabasco sauce. Pour over the ribs. Return to the oven for another 1½ hours or until tender. The meat usually releases from the bone at the end of the baking time.

GLAZED HAM STEAK

½ c. red currant jelly
¼ c. chopped onion
2 Tbsp. prepared
   mustard
1 inch thick ham
   steak, fully cooked

Combine jelly, onion, and mustard; set aside. Cook ham in skillet for 10 minutes; remove. Add jelly mixture and melt. Add ham. Cook for 2 minutes on each side. Spoon sauce over ham to serve.

HAM LOAF

2 lb. ground ham
1 lb. ground pork butt
4 crackers, soaked in
   ½ c. milk
3 beaten eggs

Mix and shape in loaf. Bake 2 hours at 350°. Baste often.

BAKED HAM WITH PEACH GLAZE

Ham
Peach preserves

Bake ham at 325°, allowing 20 minutes baking time for each pound of weight. Bake with fat side up. Last 15 minutes of baking time, take ham out of oven and trim off fat, then spread ½ cup peach preserves over ham. Bake remaining 15 minutes or until well glazed.

BREADS, ROLLS, PASTRIES

BLUEBERRY-ORANGE BREAD

2 eggs
1 c. milk
1 pkg. orange muffin
mix
1 pkg. blueberry
muffin mix

Mix with fork. Bake in a greased loaf pan at 350° for 50 to 60 minutes.

CRUSTY FRENCH BREAD

1 pkg. dry yeast
1¾ c. lukewarm
water
1 Tbsp. sugar
2 tsp. salt
4 c. flour

Dissolve yeast, sugar, and salt in lukewarm water. Add flour. Cover and let rise until double in bulk. Leave it in the bowl and pound hard with a closed fist 18 to 20 times. Divide in ½ and put into 2 greased (bottom) 1 quart round Pyrex casseroles. Cover with a towel and let rise again. Drizzle about 2 tablespoons melted butter on each casserole. Bake in preheated oven at 400° for about 40 minutes.

This bread freezes well and reheats well in foil.

CHEESE BREAD

3⅓ c. Bisquick
1¼ c. milk
2½ c. grated cheese
2 eggs

Mix Bisquick and cheese. Beat eggs; add to milk. Pour into Bisquick and cheese mixture. Mix well. Pour into a large greased and floured pan. Bake for 50 minutes at 350°. *Best served hot.*

BANANA NUT BREAD

1 box nut bread mix
3 mashed bananas
¼ c. chopped nuts

Prepare nut bread as package directs. Stir in bananas and nuts. Bake as directed on package.

BROCCOLI CORN BREAD

2 pkg. corn muffin
   mix
10 oz. chopped
   broccoli
1 c. cottage cheese
4 eggs
1½ sticks melted
   butter

Mix together in large mixing bowl and pour into 9x13 inch dish. Bake at 350° for 35 minutes.

SOUR CREAM BREAD

1 c. self-rising corn
   meal
1 small can cream
   style corn
   (approx. 1 c.)
1 small box sour
   cream (approx. 1 c.)
2 whole eggs, beaten
½ tsp. salt

Use a small bread pan or skillet. Melt 1 stick of butter in the pan, making sure the pan is well greased, then add the melted butter to the preceding, then put mix in pan. Bake at 350° to 400° for 30 to 40 minutes.

GINGER ALE BREAD

3 c. self-rising flour
2 Tbsp. sugar
1½ c. ginger ale

Combine and mix well. Pour into a greased loaf pan and bake in a preheated 375° oven for 45 minutes.

CHEESE TWISTS

14 oz. pkg. frozen
   puff pastry,
   thawed
1 egg, beaten
¼ c. grated Romano
   cheese

Preheat oven to 450°F. Roll pastry to a thickness of ¼ inch on a lightly floured surface. Brush with beaten egg and sprinkle with cheese. Cut the pastry crosswise into strips ½ inch wide. Cut to desired lengths. Twist strips several times and place on an ungreased baking sheet, pressing down the ends to prevent the pastry from unrolling. Bake in oven 8 to 10 minutes or until golden. Makes 8 servings.

PINEAPPLE MUFFINS

2 c. Bisquick
1 (8 oz.) can crushed
  pineapple
2 Tbsp. melted butter
1 beaten egg
½ c. sugar

Mix together and bake in greased muffin tins at 400° for 20 to 25 minutes.

PULL APART ROLL

4 pkg. canned
  biscuits
1 stick butter, melted
1 c. sugar
1 tsp. cinnamon
1 c. chopped nuts

Shape biscuits into balls. Dip in melted butter, then in sugar mixture of sugar, nuts, and cinnamon. Arrange balls in layer in a greased Bundt pan. Bake at 375° for 45 minutes to 1 hour.

HUNGRY JACK BUTTER ROLL

1 big can (10) Hungry
  Jack biscuits
½ lb. real butter
3 c. sugar

Roll each biscuit real thin; spread with butter and sprinkle with 1 cup of the sugar. Sprinkle with cinnamon. Roll each biscuit (jelly roll style) and cut in half. Place in 9x12 inch pan or casserole. Melt rest of sugar (2 cups) in about 2½ cups boiling water (more if needed). Pour over rolls. Be sure to have enough water to cover well. Bake until brown.

CHEESE ROLLS

1 c. (2 sticks)
  margarine
12 oz. ctn. cottage
  cheese (small
  curd)
2 c. flour
Dash of salt

Cream margarine and cottage cheese. When fluffy, add flour and salt. Chill overnight. Divide into thirds. Roll into a circle and cut into 12 wedges. Roll up and bake for 20 to 25 minutes in a 350° oven. Drizzle with powdered sugar icing.

MAYONNAISE ROLLS

2 c. self-rising flour
1 c. milk
4 Tbsp. mayonnaise

Combine, mix and pour into greased muffin tins. Bake at 400°F. for 22 minutes.

ROSEMARY BISCUITS

2¼ c. Bisquick mix
⅔ c. milk
Melted butter
Rosemary

Mix together well. If dough is too sticky, add additional Bisquick mix to make dough easy to handle. Turn out on floured board. Shape into smooth ball and roll out to about ¼ inch thick. Cut with 2 inch biscuit cutter. Place on lightly greased baking sheet. Reserve half of the biscuits. Brush those in pan with melted butter and sprinkle lightly with crushed rosemary (dried). Place remaining biscuits on top of these and also brush with butter and sprinkle with dried rosemary. Bake at 450° for 8 to 10 minutes.

BUTTER ROLLS

3 Tbsp. butter
1 Tbsp. parsley flakes
1 Tbsp. sesame seeds
2 (8 oz.) pkg. crescent
   rolls
½ c. grated
   Parmesan/
   Romano cheese

Melt butter in cake pan in 350° oven. Add sesame seeds, parsley flakes, garlic powder, and ½ of the cheese. Remove roll from package. *Do not unroll.* Slice each section into 5 pieces and roll in mixture. Place in pan and sprinkle rest of cheese on top. Bake for 12 minutes.

RISE-AND-SHINE BISCUITS

1 Tbsp. sugar
⅓ c. club soda
⅓ c. sour cream
2 c. biscuit mix

Combine sugar, club soda, and sour cream in a medium bowl, stirring well. Add biscuit mix, stirring just until dry ingredients are moistened. Turn dough out onto a lightly floured surface and knead 10 to 12 times. Shape dough with hands into 6 biscuits, about 1 inch thick. Place 1 biscuit in the center of a lightly greased 8 inch round cake pan. Arrange remaining biscuits in a circle surrounding center biscuit. Bake at 450° for 16 to 18 minutes or *until golden brown.*

QUICK CARAMEL ROLLS

2 pkg. vanilla
  pudding (dry,
  not instant)
1 c. brown sugar
2 loaves frozen bread
  dough, thawed
½ c. butter
2 Tbsp. cream or milk
Cinnamon

Grease a 9x13 inch pan. Cut bread dough into marshmallow size pieces and put in pan. Sprinkle with cinnamon. Top with the following sauce: Vanilla pudding, brown sugar, butter, and cream, heated on stove long enough to mix together and melt butter. Bake at 350° about 25 minutes. Remove from oven and flip pan over so that sauce can cover rolls.

OVERNIGHT COFFEE CAKE

1 (3¼ oz.) pkg.
  vanilla pudding
  (not instant)
¾ stick butter, melted
½ c. brown sugar
½ c. chopped pecans
1 (25 oz.) bag frozen
  rolls (20 rolls)

Combine dry pudding mix with brown sugar. Place pecan pieces in well buttered Bundt pan, then place frozen rolls on top of pecans. Pour melted butter over frozen rolls and sprinkle with the pudding mix. Leave cake out overnight, covered. (Dough will rise.) Bake at 350° for 30 minutes. Invert on serving plate right away.

HERSHEY'S BAR PIE

½ c. milk
16 large
  marshmallows
1 large Hershey's bar
  with almonds
  (½ lb.)
1 c. whipped cream

Heat milk and marshmallows in top of a double boiler. Add the Hershey's bar and mix until melted and blended. Cool. Fold into the chocolate mixture the whipped cream. Pour into a graham cracker crust and chill.

PEACH PIE - ALMOST

1 (1 lb. 13 oz.) can
  peach slices,
  drained
1 c. firmly packed
  brown sugar
½ pkg. (10 oz.) pie
  crust mix
¼ c. melted butter or
  margarine

Preheat oven to 350°. Arrange peach slices in bottom of a buttered shallow baking dish. Crumble pie crust mix into a bowl. Add sugar. Mix well. Sprinkle over peaches. Top all with melted butter or margarine. Bake 25 to 30 minutes.

KEY LIME PIE

1 graham cracker
   crumb or baked
   pastry pie shell
1⅓ c. (14 oz.) can
   sweetened
   condensed milk
½ c. lime juice (Key
   West is good)
1 tsp. grated lime rind
1 c. heavy cream,
   whipped, or
   Cool Whip

Combine sweetened condensed milk, lime juice, and lime rind. Stir until well blended and thickened. Fold in ½ of the Cool Whip. Pour into chilled crumb crust or cooked pastry shell. Spread remaining Cool Whip over top of pie filling. Chill.

PEANUT BUTTER PIE

5 oz. cream cheese,
   softened
⅓ c. peanut butter
1 c. powdered sugar
9 oz. non-dairy
   whipped
   topping
Graham cracker or
   chocolate
   cookie crust

Mix cream cheese and peanut butter. Add powdered sugar and whipped topping, blending until smooth. Pour into the crust. Freeze for several hours.

PINEAPPLE CHESS PIE

1½ c. sugar
2 Tbsp. flour
1 stick margarine
2 eggs
1 flat can crushed
   pineapple

Combine sugar with sifted flour. Crumble in margarine. Beat in the 2 eggs. Add the can of crushed pineapple with juice. Pour in uncooked deep dish pie shell and bake in a 325° to 350° oven for approximately 40 minutes.

MILE HIGH STRAWBERRY PIE

10 oz. frozen
   strawberries,
   thawed
½ c. sugar
1 Tbsp. lemon juice
⅛ tsp. salt
2 egg whites

Combine all ingredients and beat no less than 15 minutes. Fold in ½ pint whipping cream, whipped with ½ teaspoon vanilla. Put in baked 10 inch pie shell; freeze until solid.

LEMONADE PIE

1 graham cracker
    crust
1 can Eagle Brand
    milk
1 small Cool Whip
1 can frozen pink
    lemonade
    (small can)
Pecans

Stir lemonade into milk; add Cool Whip and whip very well. Pour into pie shell. Sprinkle with pecans. Refrigerate.

CHOCOLATE ICE CREAM PIE

1 c. milk
1 c. vanilla ice cream,
    softened
1 pkg. instant
    chocolate
    pudding mix
1 baked pie shell

Beat together milk and ice cream. Slowly mix in pudding mix. Pour into cooled pie shell. Chill at least 4 hours. Top with whipped topping when serving if desired. (Can be frozen.)

OLD-FASHIONED MOLASSES PIE

1¼ c. molasses
¾ c. sugar
3 eggs
1 Tbsp. flour

Mix molasses and butter in pan and bring to a boil. Beat eggs. Mix flour and sugar. Add eggs and molasses mixture. Bake in a pie shell at 325° for 30 minutes.

QUICK PEACH COBBLER

½ c. sugar
½ c. milk
2 tsp. baking powder
1 c. flour
1 stick margarine

Melt margarine in baking dish. Leave enough to grease dish. Pour remaining margarine into the first 4 ingredients. Pour into buttered dish, then pour a No. 303 or larger can peaches and juice over batter. Sprinkle ½ cup sugar over top. Bake at 425° for 30 to 40 minutes.

CHEESE CAKE

1½ lb. cream cheese
1 c. sugar
4 eggs, separated
1 tsp. vanilla
1 pt. sour cream

Prepare graham cracker crust and line spring form pan. Mix cream cheese and sugar together. Add egg yolks, sour cream, and vanilla. Fold in egg whites, which have been beaten to stiff peaks. Bake at 350° for 55 minutes. Turn off oven (keep oven door closed) for 10 minutes. Open door and let cake sit for 1 hour in the oven. Top with pie filling (cherry, blueberry or strawberry).

MUD PIE

½ pkg. Nabisco
    chocolate
    wafers
½ cube butter,
    melted
1 gal. coffee ice
    cream
1½ c. fudge sauce

Crush wafers and add butter. Mix well. Press into 9 inch pie plate. Cover with soft coffee ice cream. Put into freezer until ice cream is firm. Top with cold fudge sauce (it helps to place fudge sauce in freezer for a time to make spreading easier). Store Mud Pie in freezer approximately 10 hours. Slice and top with whipped cream and slivered almonds.

FLAKY PIE CRUST

2 c. flour
¾ c. Crisco
½ tsp. salt
¼ c. cold water

Take ⅓ cup of the flour out and mix with water to make a paste. After mixing shortening in the other flour and salt, work in the paste. Bake at 400° until brown.

OATMEAL PIE CRUST

1 c. oatmeal, ground
    in blender
⅓ c. brown sugar
3 to 4 Tbsp. oleo
½ tsp. cinnamon

Bake at 375° for 8 to 10 minutes.

DESSERTS

SOUTHERN PECAN MIST CAKE

12 egg whites
1 tsp. salt
3⅛ c. sifted
  powdered
  sugar
12 egg yolks
3 c. pecans, finely
  chopped

Beat egg whites and salt until foamy. Gradually add powdered sugar and continue beating until stiff, but not dry. Beat egg yolks very carefully into the whites. Gently fold in the pecans. Pour into ungreased 10 inch tube pan. Bake at 350° for 50 minutes. Remove from oven and invert pan to cool cake before removing from pan.

EASY POUND CAKE

1 lb. butter or
  margarine
16 oz. box
  confectioners
  sugar
6 eggs
3 c. plain flour
1 Tbsp. vanilla
  flavoring

Sift flour 3 times before measuring. Cream together butter or margarine with sugar. Add flour and eggs alternately. Add vanilla. Pour into greased and floured 10 inch tube pan. Bake in a 325° oven for 1 hour or until done and a wooden toothpick inserted in center comes out clean.

FRUIT CAKE

1 (20 oz.) can crushed
  pineapple
1 (20 oz.) can cherry
  (or apple) pie
  filling
1 yellow cake mix
¾ c. melted butter
1 c. pecans

Dump pineapple and pie filling into 13x9x2 inch pan. Smooth out. Sprinkle cake mix evenly over this. Spread pecans on top. Pour butter over pecans. Bake at 350° for 1 hour. Serve in pan.

TRIPLE FUDGE CAKE

1 (3 oz.) pkg. regular
  chocolate
  pudding mix
2 c. milk
1 (18½ oz.) pkg.
  devils food cake
  mix
½ c. semi-sweet
  chocolate chips
½ c. chopped
  walnuts

Prepare pudding mix with milk as directed on package. Remove from heat; blend dry cake mix into hot pudding. Mixture will be quite thick and spongy. Pour into greased and floured 9x13 inch pan. Sprinkle with chocolate chips and nuts. Bake at 350° for 30 to 35 minutes.

ANGEL FOOD DELIGHT

1 round angel food
  cake
1 can crushed
  pineapple
1 large container
  Cool Whip
1 pkg. vanilla instant
  pudding

Cut cake into 2 or 3 layers. Drain some of juice from pineapple. Pour vanilla instant pudding over pineapple and let set for 5 minutes. Mix Cool Whip and pineapple mixture. Ice layers, top, and sides of cake. Refrigerate several hours before serving. Can be frozen.

PUMPKIN CAKE

1 white cake mix
½ can pumpkin mix
  (about 10 oz.)
Optional spices
  (cinnamon and
  ginger)

Make cake batter as directions tell you to. Add in pumpkin mix out of the can (taste batter to add as much pumpkin flavor as you want). Add whatever spices you prefer. Cinnamon and ginger are great. Bake cake about 5 minutes longer than your usual cake. Spread with cream cheese icing or powdered sugar is good sprinkled on.

CHERRY BOSTON CREAM CAKE

1 box yellow cake mix
1 pkg. vanilla
  pudding
1 can cherry pie
  filling

Bake cake according to mix instructions in 2 layers. Make pudding according to package instructions. Put pudding between layers of cake when cake has cooled. Pour cherry pie filling over cake.

LEMON-APRICOT CAKE

1 pkg. lemon cake
  mix
1 (approx. 1 lb.) can
  peeled apricots
3 eggs

Mix all together and bake in a 13x9 inch pan or 2 layer cake pans. Bake at 350° (moderate oven) for 30 to 35 minutes. When cooled, put together with lemon filling and sprinkle with powdered sugar.

DELICIOUS COCONUT CAKE

1 white cake mix
1 small can cream of
  coconut
1 can Eagle Brand
  milk
1 medium container
  Cool Whip
1 to 2 c. shredded
  coconut

Bake 1 white cake mix according to directions; let cook for 5 minutes, then punch thoroughly with a fork. Pour over cake the milk and cream of coconut. When cool, spread Cool Whip over cake and sprinkle with coconut.

MACE BUNDT CAKE

1 c. butter
2 c. sugar
5 large eggs
1¾ c. flour, stirred
  and measured
1 Tbsp. ground mace

Cream butter thoroughly, then add sugar gradually, continuing to beat until light and fluffy. Add eggs, 1 at a time, beating at least 1 minute while sifting flour and mace 3 times. Add flour to creamed mixture and beat on medium speed until blended. Spoon into Bundt pan that's been generously greased with shortening (using 3 to 4 tablespoons shortening), then dusted with flour. Bake at 350° for 45 minutes or until done. Turn out of pan immediately. Cool and serve un-iced.

CHOCOLATE MARSHMALLOW CAKE

Brownie mix
Miniature
  marshmallows
Prepared frosting

Use brownie mix following directions on box. When done, top with miniature marshmallows and melt quickly in oven and cool. Spread top with chocolate prepared frosting.

BLUEBERRY CAKE

Angel food cake mix
1 pkg. Cool Whip (use
   as directed)
1 can blueberry pie
   filling
1 large pkg. cream
   cheese,
   softened
½ c. confectioners
   sugar

Cook angel food cake per directions on package. Slice into 3 layers. Cream the cream cheese and sugar together; mix with Cool Whip. Spread Cool Whip mixture and 3 or 4 spoons of blueberry pie filling over each layer. Frost the top of the cake and let the blueberry filling dribble over the sides.

LEMON JELLO CAKE

1 box lemon or yellow
   cake mix
1 pkg. lemon jello
¾ c. oil (cooking)
¾ c. water
4 eggs

Mix all ingredients together at low speed, then beat at high speed for 3 minutes. Bake in greased 9x13 inch cake pan in 350° oven for 40 minutes. While baking, mix 2 cups powdered sugar with juice of 2 lemons. When cake is baked, still hot, poke holes with a fork all over the top of cake. Pour mixture over it.

FLUFFY CREAM CHEESE FROSTING

1 (8 oz.) cream
   cheese
1 (16 oz.)
   confectioners
   sugar
1 Tbsp. softened
   butter
1 tsp. vanilla

Combine cream cheese, sugar, butter, and vanilla. Mix on high speed until smooth and fluffy. Add about 1 tablespoon buttermilk (or more) to make frosting of spreading consistency.

CARAMEL ICING

1 box light brown
   sugar
⅓ stick butter
1 small can
   evaporated
   milk

Bring sugar, milk, and butter to a hard boil and thicken to spreading consistency with powdered sugar.

CHOCOLATE-BUTTER SAUCE

½ c. sugar
2 Tbsp. cocoa or 1 oz.
 baking chocolate
2 Tbsp. butter
½ c. evaporated milk

Melt chocolate over hot water. Add the butter. Stir well. Pour in milk and let cook for a few minutes, stirring all the time, then add sugar. If cocoa is used, add it to the butter and milk. Cook gently for a few minutes. Add a dash of salt.

BOILED WHITE FUDGE FROSTING

3 c. granulated sugar
1½ c. whipping
 cream
1½ Tbsp. butter
1½ tsp. vanilla

Cook sugar and cream on high until mixture comes to a boil. Turn down heat to medium low. Cook and stir until mixture reaches soft ball stage. Remove from heat; stir in butter and vanilla. Beat until creamy and thick.

1 MINUTE CHOCOLATE FROSTING

1 c. sugar
¼ c. cocoa
¼ c. butter
¼ c. milk
1 tsp. vanilla

Mix together. Bring to a boil and boil for 1 minute. Add vanilla. Cool partially, then beat.

ORANGE CREAM CHEESE FROSTING

1 (3 oz.) pkg. soft
 cream cheese
1 Tbsp. soft
 margarine
½ tsp. grated orange
 peel
1½ c. powdered
 sugar

Mix together until smooth. Add a small amount of milk to thin if needed.

PEANUT BUTTER GRANOLA BARS

¼ c. honey
⅔ c. peanut butter
3 c. granola

Butter a 9x9 inch pan. Boil honey for 1 to 2 minutes. Mix in peanut butter; add granola and press into pan. Cool and cut into bars.

CHOW MEIN COOKIES

1 pkg. chocolate bits
1 pkg. butterscotch
  bits
1 can chow mein
  noodles
1 c. chopped nuts
  (optional)

Melt chocolate and butterscotch bits in top of double boiler. Remove from heat and stir in noodles and nuts. Drop by spoonfuls onto waxed paper. Cool.

SPICY OATMEAL RAISIN COOKIES

1 pkg. Duncan Hines
  spice cake mix
4 egg whites
1 c. quick cooking
  oats (not instant or old-
  fashioned)
½ c. Crisco oil
½ c. raisins

Heat oven to 350°. Grease baking sheets. Combine cake mix, egg whites, oats, raisins, and oil in large bowl. Mix on low speed of electric mixer until blended. Drop from rounded teaspoons onto baking sheet. Bake at 350° for 7 to 9 minutes. Cool for 1 minute on baking sheet. Remove to cooling rack.

BUTTER COOKIES

1 c. butter
½ c. white sugar
2 tsp. vanilla
2 c. flour, sifted

Soften butter, then add in mixture of sugar and vanilla. Mix together, then add in sifted flour; knead the dough, then roll it with a rolling pin. Make dough into little balls and flatten into cookies. Bake at 310° for about 25 minutes.

MELTS

2 egg whites
¾ c. sugar
6 oz. pkg. chocolate
  chips
½ c. chopped
  walnuts
  (optional)

Heat oven to 375°. Beat egg whites until foamy; add sugar and beat until stiff. Fold in chips and nuts. Drop by mounds onto greased cookie sheet. Place in oven and turn heat off. Leave cookies in oven until cold.

EASY CUTOUT COOKIES

1 box yellow cake mix
¼ c. oil
1 Tbsp. water
1 egg

Mix all ingredients. Roll to ¼ inch and cut. Bake 6 minutes at 350°.

PUDDING COOKIES

1 box cake mix
  (chocolate or
  other)
1 c. sour cream
1 pkg. instant
  pudding
  (chocolate or other)
2 eggs

Mix all ingredients. Makes a very stiff batter. Drop by teaspoon on greased cookie sheet. Bake at 350° for 8 to 10 minutes. Frost with chocolate or other flavored frosting. *Makes very moist cookies.* If desired, top with a half walnut.

GRAHAM CRACKER CHEWS

1 pkg. graham
  crackers
½ c. brown sugar
½ c. margarine
½ c. chopped
  walnuts

Line a greased 15x10 inch cookie sheet with crackers. Bring to boil ½ cup brown sugar and ½ cup margarine. Pour over crackers. Sprinkle top with nuts. Bake at 350° for 10 minutes only. Cool in refrigerator; separate into bars.

UNBELIEVABLE COOKIES

1 c. sugar
1 egg
1 c. peanut butter
  (smooth or crunchy)
½ tsp. vanilla

Mix all together. Roll into small balls and put on cookie sheet. Flatten with a fork. Bake until real light brown at 350°.

COCONUT JOYS

½ c. butter
2 c. powdered sugar
3 c. coconut (8 oz.)
2 oz. semi-sweet
  chocolate chips,
  melted

Melt butter in saucepan. Remove from heat. Add powdered sugar and coconut. Mix well. Shape a rounded teaspoonful of mixture into balls. Flatten slightly by making an indentation in the center of each. Place them on a cookie sheet. Fill centers with the melted chocolate. Place an almond sliver or half on the top (optional). Chill until firm. Store in refrigerator.

PECAN COOKIES

1 c. butter
2 c. brown sugar
2 whole eggs
3 c. flour
2 c. chopped pecans

Mix well and drop with teaspoon on baking tin. Top with ½ pecan. Bake in moderate oven about 10 minutes.

ALMOND BUTTER COOKIES

1 c. butter
½ c. sugar
1 tsp. almond extract
2 c. flour
¼ tsp. salt (optional)

Cream butter and sugar. Add extract. Add flour and salt. Chill dough. Form 1 inch balls and roll in sugar. Flatten with cookie stamp or back of spoon. Bake at 350° for 10 to 12 minutes.

SNOWBALL COOKIES

1 c. butter or
  margarine
2 c. ground pecans
2 c. flour
4 Tbsp. granulated
  sugar
1 tsp. vanilla

Cream butter. Add sugar and remaining ingredients. Roll into small balls. Bake at 325° for 30 minutes. Roll into powdered sugar when hot and again when cold.

CHOCOLATE RITZ DIPPED COOKIES

1 (1 lb.) block
  chocolate or
  chips of chocolate
1 box Ritz crackers
1 jar peanut butter
  (creamy)

Melt chocolate in double boiler or micro-wave. Spread peanut butter between 2 Ritz crackers. Dip crackers in chocolate (coat all of crackers with chocolate). Place on waxed paper and let cool. Chocolate will harden.

DATE-NUT BALLS

1 stick margarine
1 c. sugar
1 small box dates,
  pitted
1 egg
1 tsp. vanilla

Mix all together in a large saucepan. Over low heat, cook for about 10 minutes or until dates have melted and mixture is smooth. Remove from heat; add 2 cups chopped nuts and 2 cups Rice Krispies. Make into balls about the size of walnuts and roll in powdered sugar.

BUTTERSCOTCH ROUNDS

½ c. Karo dark corn
  syrup
¼ c. margarine
¾ c. sugar

Combine ingredients in heavy 1 quart sauce-pan. Cook over medium heat, stirring con-stantly, until sugar is dissolved and mixture comes to a boil. Continue cooking, stirring occasionally, until temperature reaches 270°F. or until drops of syrup separate into hard, but not brittle, threads in cold water. Remove from heat. Drop by teaspoonfuls onto greased baking sheet.

FROZEN PEANUT-BUTTER CUPS

1 c. whipping cream
1 (7 oz.) jar
  marshmallow
  cream
1 (3 oz.) pkg. cream
  cheese,
  softened
½ c. chunky peanut
  butter
Chocolate curls (to
  garnish)

Beat whipping cream until stiff peaks form. In large bowl with same beaters, beat at low speed marshmallow cream, cream cheese, and peanut butter until smooth. With rubber spatula, fold whipped cream into peanut-butter mixture. Line muffin cups, 2½ x 1¼ inches, with fluted paper or foil baking cups. Cover; freeze at least 3 hours or more, until firm. To serve, garnish with chocolate curls.

PEANUT CLUSTERS

12 oz. chocolate
   chips
12 oz. Reese's peanut
   butter chips
2 c. salted peanuts

Combine and heat on HIGH in microwave for 2½ to 3 minutes or until melted. Stir in peanuts. Drop by clusters onto waxed paper. Chill to set.

PEANUT BUTTER FUDGE

2 c. sugar
⅔ c. milk
1 c. peanut butter
1 c. marshmallow
   cream
1 tsp. vanilla

Cook sugar and milk to soft ball stage. Add peanut butter, marshmallow cream, and vanilla. Stir until dissolved. Pour into 8x8 inch square Pyrex buttered dish. Let stand until firm.

BELGIAN FUDGE

1 can condensed milk
1 c. granulated sugar
½ stick butter
1 tsp. vanilla
1 c. chopped pecans

Cook milk and sugar on low flame until it shows signs of sugaring and is caramel color; stir constantly. Just before removing from fire, add butter and nuts. Pour into greased pan and cut into squares.

FUDGEMALLOW RAISIN CANDY

1 (12 oz.) pkg.
   Baker's semi-
   sweet chocolate
   chips
1 c. chunky peanut
   butter
3 c. Kraft
   marshmallows
¾ c. raisins

Microwave chocolate and peanut butter in 2 quart bowl on 50% for 2 to 3 minutes or until melted, stirring occasionally. Fold in raisins and marshmallows. Pour into foil-lined 8 inch square pans. Chill.

APRICOT BALLS

1 (8 oz.) pkg. dried
   apricots,
   ground or finely cut
   up
2½ c. flaked coconut
¾ c. sweetened
   condensed milk
⅔ c. finely chopped
   nuts

Mix apricots, coconut, and milk. Shape mixture into 1 inch balls; roll each in nuts. Let stand until firm, about 2 hours.

PEANUT BRITTLE

Microwave.

1 c. raw peanuts
1 c. sugar
½ c. white Karo
⅛ tsp. salt

Stir these ingredients together in 8 cup measure. Place in microwave and cook on HIGH for 7 to 8 minutes, stirring after 4 minutes. Add 1 teaspoon oleo and 1 teaspoon vanilla. Return to microwave and cook 1 minute more. Peanuts will be lightly browned and syrup very hot. Add 1 teaspoon soda and gently stir until light and foamy. Pour and spread onto lightly greased cookie sheet. Let cool ½ hour, then break into pieces.

REESE'S

1½ c. crushed
   graham
   crackers
1 lb. box powdered
   sugar
1½ c. peanut butter
2 sticks butter,
   melted
1 (12 oz.) pkg.
   chocolate chips

Combine graham crackers, powdered sugar, and peanut butter. Mix well. Add melted butter. Spread mixture into 9x13 inch pan. Melt one 12 ounce package chocolate chips. Spread over peanut butter mixture. Set in refrigerator. Cut into squares when chilled. Very rich.

BAKED PECANS

1 lb. pecans
1 egg white
½ c. sugar
½ tsp. cinnamon
½ tsp. salt

Toss pecans with egg white and 1 teaspoon cold water; beat until frothy. Mix sugar, salt, and cinnamon. Toss pecans in mixture until well coated. Bake at 225° on buttered cookie sheet for 1 hour. Stir every 15 minutes.

CORN FLAKE TREATS

½ box brown sugar
1 c. light Karo syrup
1 c. peanut butter
1 c. butter
1 (12 oz.) box corn
flakes

Heat first 4 ingredients to boil. Remove from heat and add corn flakes. Spread on prepared pan or cookie sheet. (Prepare pan by coating with Pam or butter for easy cutting and removing.)

JIFFY BROWNIES

1 pkg. chocolate cake
mix
3 eggs
1 can cherry pie
filling mix
1 tsp. almond extract

Place cake mix (dry) into mixing bowl. Beat well 3 eggs; add to dry mix. Add can of pie filling mix. Stir well. Add 1 teaspoon of almond extract. Mix well. Spread onto greased jelly roll pan. Bake at 350° for 20 minutes. Allow to cool and serve with whipped cream.

CHOCOLATE CHIP COOKIE PIZZA

1 roll chocolate chip
regular cookie
dough
1 pkg. real chocolate
chips
1 c. chopped pecans
1 jar caramel topping

Spread cookie dough on pizza pan. Bake as directed. Remove from oven and immediately put ½ of chocolate chips and ½ pecans on top. Spread caramel topping and sprinkle the rest of chocolate chips and pecans on top.

APPLE CRISP

2 cans pie sliced
  apples
1½ c. flour
1 c. sugar
½ c. brown sugar
½ c. oleo

In a 13x9 inch buttered dish, place 2 cans of pie sliced apples. Sprinkle ¾ cup of sugar over apples. Mix together 1½ cups flour, ½ cup brown sugar, ½ cup oleo, and ¼ cup sugar. Sprinkle mixture over apples. Bake 60 minutes at 350°.

CREME DE MENTHE PARFAIT

1 c. creme de menthe
2 (3 oz.) pkg. lemon
  Jell-O
1 pt. whipping cream

Dissolve Jell-O in 2 cups hot water. Add 1 cup cold water and creme de menthe. Let set in mixing bowl until partially jelled. Pour whipping cream in Jell-O and beat a long time. Pour into parfait glasses. Makes 8 servings.

FROZEN DESSERT

1 pkg. slice and bake
  cookies
½ gal. vanilla ice
  cream,
  softened
1 (8 oz.) jar
  butterscotch
  topping

Bake cookies as directed on package; let cool. Combine ice cream and topping. Line cake pan with cookies. Spread ice cream mixture over cookies. Sprinkle with extra cookie crumbs. Freeze. Slice.

HEAVENLY RICE PUDDING

3 c. half & half
¼ c. sugar
2 c. cooked rice (not
  Minute rice)
2 Tbsp. butter or
  margarine
1 tsp. vanilla extract

Combine all the ingredients in a medium size heavy saucepan. Simmer 20 to 30 minutes or until thick. Pour into 4 or 5 small custard cups. Serve warm or cold. Makes 4 to 5 servings.

PUDDING DELIGHT

14 whole graham
  crackers
1 (6 serving size) pkg.
  Jell-O instant
  vanilla pudding mix
2 c. cold milk
1 to 1½ c. thawed
  Cool Whip
1 (21 oz.) can cherry
  pie filling

Line a 9 inch square pan with whole graham crackers, breaking crackers if necessary. Prepare pudding mix with milk as directed on package (use only 2 cups milk, not 3, as shown on package). Let stand 5 minutes, then blend in whipped topping. Spread half of the pudding mixture over the crackers. Add another layer of crackers. Top with remaining pudding mixture and one more layer of crackers. Spread cherry pie filling over top of crackers. Chill at least 3 hours before serving.

LAYERED PUDDING

1 box chocolate
  pudding (not
  instant)
1 box vanilla pudding
  (not instant)
1 pkg. graham
  crackers

Cook pudding according to directions. While hot, place in 8x8 inch glass dish as follows: Layer of vanilla pudding, graham crackers, chocolate pudding, and graham crackers, etc. Sprinkle top layer with graham crackers. Refrigerate for at least 6 hours.

BANANA PUDDING

1 large vanilla instant
  pudding and
  pie mix
1 large Cool Whip
1 can sweetened
  condensed milk
Bananas and vanilla
  wafers

Mix pudding and pie filling mix as per package directions; fold in condensed milk and Cool Whip. Layer bananas and vanilla wafers and pudding mix until pudding mix is all gone. Makes a very large banana pudding.

WHITE BROWNIES

1 white cake mix (2
  layer)
⅓ c. brown sugar
⅓ c. milk
1 egg
6 oz. butterscotch or
  chocolate chip
  morsels

Stir all ingredients, except chips, until moistened. Add chips. Bake in 9x13 inch (greased) pan at 325° for 30 minutes.

Note: You can use a 12 ounce package of chips if desired.

LEMON CHEESE BARS

1 Duncan Hines
   pudding
   recipe yellow cake
   mix
1 (8 oz.) pkg. cream
   cheese,
   softened
⅓ c. sugar
1 tsp. lemon juice

Mix dry cake mix, 1 egg and ⅓ cup oil until crumbly; reserve 1 cup. Pat remaining mixture lightly in ungreased 13x9x2 inch pan. Bake 15 minutes at 350°. Beat cheese, sugar, lemon juice, and 1 egg until light and smooth. Spread over baked layer. Sprinkle with reserved crumb mixture. Bake 15 minutes longer. Cool; cut into bars.

PISTACHIO DESSERT

9 oz. Cool Whip
3¾ oz. pkg. pistachio
   pudding
2 c. mini
   marshmallows
1 c. coconut
1 can crushed
   pineapple and
   juice

Mix and set in refrigerator.

TWINKIE SURPRISE

1 pkg. (10) Twinkies
1 box vanilla instant
   pudding
1½ c. milk
1 (8 oz.) pkg. Cool
   Whip
2 boxes frozen
   strawberries (in sugar),
   thawed

Slice Twinkies in halves lengthwise. Put in 13x9x1 inch pan. Pour thawed strawberries over Twinkies. In a large bowl, mix pudding, milk, and Cool Whip. Pour over the strawberries. Cover with Saran Wrap and let stand in refrigerator overnight.

CHERRY FLUFF

1 can cherry pie
  filling
1 can crushed
  pineapple
1 pkg. chopped
  pecans
1 can Eagle Brand
  milk
1 large ctn. Cool
  Whip

Open all of the cans; drain the pineapple and mix all the ingredients in a large bowl. Cool and serve.

MISCELLANEOUS

BAKED HAM SANDWICHES

¼ c. butter, softened
1½ tsp. prepared
  mustard
4 hamburger buns
4 thin slices ham
4 thin slices Swiss
  cheese

Combine butter and mustard; spread on hamburger buns. Place slice of ham and slice of cheese on each bun. Wrap each separately in foil or place in baking pan and cover with foil. Bake at 350° for 20 minutes or until heated through.

CREAMY NUTTY TUNA SANDWICHES

1 (8 oz.) pkg.
  Philadelphia
  cream cheese
½ c. mayonnaise
2 Tbsp. lemon juice
1 c. flaked tuna
½ c. ripe olives,
  chopped

Blend together cream cheese, lemon juice, and mayonnaise. Fold in chopped olives and flaked tuna. Season. Spread all slices of bread with butter. Spread with filling. Cut edges from sandwiches and cut in triangles. Butter edges and dip in chopped pecans. Garnish with sweet pickle sticks and potato chips. Place in freezer until needed.

ORANGE-NUT SANDWICH

4 oz. cream cheese
1 Tbsp. grated
  orange rind
¼ c. chopped raisins
2 Tbsp. chopped
  pecans
2 Tbsp. orange juice

Put pecans in blender and chop. Add other ingredients and mix well until consistency is easily spreadable.

SPINACH STACK-UPS

1 small box frozen
  spinach
½ c. sour cream
½ c. Ranch dressing
6 slices bacon, fried
  and crumbled
24 (6 inch) flour
  tortillas

Thaw spinach; squeeze until water is removed. Combine sour cream, dressing, and crumbled bacon until smooth. Add to spinach and mix well. Spread filling on flour tortilla; top with another tortilla.

These should be made like a sandwich. Stack filled sandwiches on top of each other; cut through stack with a sharp knife into quarters.

OPEN-FACED SANDWICH

Toasted English
  muffin
Ham
Chicken breast
Swiss cheese
Thousand Island
  salad dressing

On muffin, spread dressing. Layer with slice of chicken, ham, and cheese. Put under broiler until cheese melts.

SWEET SANDWICH

⅓ c. orange juice
1 small pkg. cream
  cheese
¾ c. dates, chopped
⅓ c. pecans

Use blender; chop pecans. Add orange juice and cream cheese which has been cut into pieces. Lastly, add dates and mix well.

FRENCH TOASTED SANDWICHES

4 thin slices ham (to
  fit bread)
4 thin slices cheese
  (to fit bread)
8 slices buttered
  bread
2 eggs, slightly
  beaten
½ c. milk or cream
Butter

Place slice of ham and cheese between 2 slices bread making 4 sandwiches. Combine eggs and milk. Dip sandwiches in egg mixture. Brown on both sides in heavy skillet or on grill, using butter as needed. Makes 4 sandwiches.

SLOPPY JOE MIX

2 lb. ground chuck
2 cans tomato soup
2 or 3 stalks celery
Medium to large
   green pepper
Medium to large
   onion

Brown the ground chuck and season with 1 teaspoon salt and ¼ teaspoon pepper per pound of meat. Add chopped onion, green pepper, and celery. Simmer until vegetables soften. Add 1½ cans of soup and 3 to 4 ounces of water. Bring to a boil, stirring quite a bit. Turn burner to simmer and cook for 30 minutes, stirring every 10 minutes.

ZIPPY HAM AND CHEESE SPREAD

½ lb. grated cheese
½ c. deviled ham
¼ c. evaporated milk
¼ c. pickle relish
1 tsp. prepared
   mustard

Mix cheese, ham, milk, relish, and mustard. Spread over bread slices. Top with lettuce and a second bread slice.

OPEN FACED TOAST 'N' EGGS

1 slice bread
1 (1 oz.) slice
   Provolone
   cheese
1 poached egg

About 10 minutes before serving, toast bread, then top it with cheese. Place on a cookie sheet and heat in a 350° oven until cheese just melts. Top with poached egg.

PLAIN OMELET

3 Tbsp. butter or
   margarine
3 Tbsp. water
½ tsp. salt
Dash of pepper
6 eggs

Beat your eggs well; add seasonings and water. Mix again. Melt butter or margarine in a pan over moderate heat. Pour eggs into pan. As eggs set, lift up edges and tip the pan so that uncooked eggs flow under the cooked portion. When bottom is browned and eggs are set, fold over halfway and slip omelet onto a hot serving platter.

Chopped ham may be added, as well as cheese, while cooking the omelet.

EGG-SAUSAGE SOUFFLE

6 slices cubed bread
1 lb. loose sausage,
   browned and drained
6 beaten eggs
1 tsp. dry mustard
2 c. milk

Layer the following in a 9x14 inch casserole:

First layer - Use 6 slices bread.

Second layer - Use 1 pound sausage.

Third layer - Combine eggs, dry mustard, and 2 cups milk. Cover; refrigerate for 12 hours or overnight. Bake at 350° for 45 to 60 minutes.

JALAPENO QUICHE

1 (11 oz.) pickled
   jalapeno
   peppers
10 oz. sharp
   Cheddar,
   shredded
4 eggs, beaten

Line glass pie pan with peppers. You may remove the seeds if you do not want this to be piquant. Put cheese over peppers (higher in the middle). Slowly pour beaten eggs over cheese. Bake at 275° for 45 minutes.

CHILE QUICHE

2 (4 oz.) cans whole
   green chiles
12 oz. Monterey Jack
   cheese, grated
4 eggs
1 tsp. Worcestershire
   sauce

Drain chiles; cut in halves and remove seeds. Line a 9 inch pan with chiles. Place grated cheese over chiles. Beat eggs with Worcestershire sauce. Pour over cheese. Bake at 275° for 45 minutes or until set.

BUTTERY FRENCH TOAST

2 eggs, beaten
1 c. milk
⅛ tsp. salt
4 slices bread

In a mixing bowl, mix eggs, milk, and salt until well blended. Place slice of fresh bread briefly in mixture, covering both sides. Cook in skillet, using butter for cooking oil. Brown lightly on both sides. Cook on low to medium heat. Serve with butter melted on top, then add sugar and cinnamon or syrup.

BREAKFAST SURPRISE

1 (8½ oz.) box corn
bread mix
1 (7 oz.) pkg. Brown
and Serve
sausage
1 (29 oz.) can sliced
peaches,
drained

Prepare corn bread batter according to package directions. Set aside.

Brown sausage and cut links into fourths. Arrange peaches and sausage on bottom of 9 inch square dish sprayed with vegetable spray. Pour corn bread batter over top. Bake at 375° about 25 minutes or until toothpick inserted in corn bread comes out clean. Cut in squares and serve upside-down with the peaches and sausage on top. *Good with syrup.*

CHEESE STRATA

1 loaf white bread
1 lb. Italian style
sausage
12 eggs
1 c. milk (plus more
as needed)
2 c. Cheddar cheese

Cut bread into cubes and spread in a 9x13 inch baking dish. Fry sausage; drain. Spread over bread cubes. Beat 12 eggs; add milk. Pour over sausage. Add more milk to almost fill dish. Sprinkle cheese over top. Bake 1 hour at 350°.

EGG AND BACON PIE

6 oz. puff pastry
4 to 5 eggs
¼ lb. bacon
1 Tbsp. chopped
parsley
Salt and pepper to
taste

Divide puff pastry into halves. Roll out 1 portion and line a pie dish, glazing the edges with milk. Remove rind from bacon and cut into small pieces. Place ½ of the bacon on the pastry lining and crack eggs on top of bacon. Season with salt and pepper; sprinkle with parsley. Put remainder of bacon on top of eggs. Roll out remaining pastry. Cover pie and press edges together. Glaze with milk. Prick top with fork and put into a hot (475°F.) oven for about 30 minutes, decreasing heat throughout (every 10 minutes).

EASY FRITOS PIE

1 large pkg. Fritos,
  crushed
1 large can chili
½ medium onion,
  chopped
1 c. grated cheese

Combine Fritos, chili, onion, and ½ cup cheese on top. Bake in a 350° oven for about 25 to 30 minutes or until bubbling.

PITA TOAST WITH GARLIC

Use with steak or chicken dinners.

2 large pita pockets
3 Tbsp. butter
2 Tbsp. olive oil
2 tsp. minced garlic
1 tsp. thyme

Preheat broiler. Split pita pockets into 4 rounds, then each round in half. Arrange, cut side up, on cookie sheet.

In small skillet, melt butter. Add olive oil and garlic; saute for 30 seconds. Brush butter evenly over bread and sprinkle with thyme. Broil until crisp, about 1 to 1½ minutes.

WELSH RAREBIT

1 egg
¼ tsp. salt
⅛ tsp. paprika
2 Tbsp. milk
½ c. grated cheese

Beat eggs into top of small double boiler. Beat until foamy. Stir in other ingredients until smooth and thick. Pour over toast and serve immediately.

CREAM OF MUSHROOM GRAVY

3 Tbsp. flour
3 Tbsp. butter
2 c. milk
2 cans cream of
  mushroom
  soup or 1 c.
  mushrooms,
  sauteed in butter
Salt to taste

Heat butter in skillet over low heat; stir in flour quickly. Make into a paste; add milk, a little at a time, stirring constantly, then pour in mushroom soup. Heat thoroughly. Serve in separate bowl to put over rice.

MACARONI AND CHEESE

2 c. elbow macaroni
1 tsp. salt
8 slices cheese,
  broken into small
  pieces
2/3 c. milk
Pepper to taste

Cook macaroni in boiling, salted water until tender; drain, then add cheese, milk, salt, and pepper. Mix. Bake in 8x8x2 inch pan for 25 minutes at 400°F. Cover with cheese slices (your choice) before serving while still hot.

CHEESY MACARONI AND HAM

1 large box Kraft
  deluxe
  macaroni and
  cheese
1 can cream of
  mushroom soup
1 can chunk ham,
  flaked

Cook macaroni and cheese according to package directions. Add soup and ham; mix well. Put mixture into small baking dish. Bake at 350° for 20 to 25 minutes.

MACARONI AND CHEESE CASSEROLE DELUXE

1 pkg. macaroni and
  cheese
10 oz. frozen or fresh
  broccoli
1 lb. ground beef or
  sausage
1 can celery soup

Cook macaroni as directed. Cook broccoli till tender-crisp. Brown ground beef or sausage. Mix all 3 and pour into greased baking dish. Top with soup and bake at 350° for 30 minutes. Top with package of dry cheese mixture the last 15 minutes.

E-Z PIZZA

1 pkg. English
  muffins
16 oz. spaghetti
  sauce
1 pkg. cheese,
  shredded or
  sliced

Preheat oven to 350°. Separate muffins. Spread large spoon of sauce on top of each half muffin. Spread cheese on top. Bake in oven for 10 minutes or until cheese is melted.

MANICOTTI CASSEROLE

10 to 12 manicotti
  noodles
Monterey Jack
  cheese, grated
Swiss cheese, grated
Mozzarella cheese,
  grated
Prego meat spaghetti
  sauce

Cook manicotti noodles as directed on package. Let cool. Stuff with grated cheeses. Place manicotti in dish and cover with spaghetti sauce. Bake at 350° until cheese melts and is hot.

QUICK MICROWAVE NACHOS

1 (7 oz.) bag tortilla
  chips
1 (16 oz.) can chilli
  without beans
2 c. shredded
  Monterey
  Jack cheese (with
  or without
  jalapeno peppers
  to taste)

Layer chips, chilli, and cheese on nonmetal plate or shallow bowl. Microwave on HIGH for 1 minute or until cheese is melted.

RAVIOLI CASSEROLE

40 oz. can ravioli
8 oz. sour cream
10 oz. thawed
  broccoli
1 c. shredded
  Mozzarella
  cheese

Place broccoli on oiled baking dish. Mix sour cream and ravioli. Pour on top of broccoli. Sprinkle cheese on top. Bake at 375° for 20 minutes.

FETTUCCINE ALFREDO

1 pkg. extra long
  fettuccine
¼ lb. real butter
½ c. grated
  Parmesan
  cheese
⅔ c. light cream
1 egg yolk

Cook noodles according to directions. While noodles are cooking, beat egg yolk lightly with fork and add to cream. Melt butter. Place drained, hot noodles in warm serving bowl. Pour over the noodles the egg and cream mixture, melted butter, and half the Parmesan cheese. Toss until well blended, adding rest of cheese while tossing. Serve immediately. Add small boiled shrimp if desired.

HOMEMADE NOODLES

1 beaten egg
½ tsp. salt
2 Tbsp. evaporated
  milk
1 c. flour

Combine egg, salt, and milk. Add enough flour to make stiff dough. Roll very thin on floured surface. Let stand 20 minutes. Roll up and slice ⅛ inch thick; spread out and dry 2 hours.

BEEF JERKY

1 (3 to 5 lb.) piece
  flank steak
Salt
Coarsely ground
  pepper
3 cloves minced
  garlic

Place meat in freezer and allow it to freeze halfway, so that ice crystals are visible, but meat is slightly pliable. Using your hands, tear off thin strips of meat along the grain. Pound meat slightly with flat side of a wooden spoon. Place meat on a rack in a baking pan. Lightly salt meat and heavily pepper both sides. Rub with minced garlic. Cook at 200°, turning once, for 6 hours. Store in airtight jar in a dark place.

BAKED POTATO TOPPING

1 (11 oz.) can
  Cheddar soup
1 c. broccoli
  flowerets
2 Tbsp. sour cream
¼ tsp. Dijon mustard
4 large baked
  potatoes

Steam broccoli flowerets until tender. In 1½ quart saucepan, stir soup over medium heat. Stir in broccoli, sour cream, and mustard. Heat thoroughly. Stir occasionally. Split potatoes and fluff with fork. Serve sauce over potatoes.

CRUMB TOPPING

1 c. flour
½ c. butter
½ c. sugar (white or
brown)

Cut butter into flour and sugar; mix until size of pea. Sprinkle on top of filling. Bake according to pie crust directions.

Can be used as topping on any fruit pie.

CARAMEL PECAN APPLES

4 apples
1 (6 oz.) bag caramels
4 sticks
3 Tbsp. water
1½ c. chopped
pecans

Wash and dry apples. Insert sticks into stem end. Melt caramels with water in a heavy saucepan. When melted, dip apples into caramel and shake off excess caramel. Roll into chopped pecans.

APPLESAUCE

4 medium size
apples, pared
and cored
1 c. water
½ c. brown sugar
¼ tsp. cinnamon
⅛ tsp. nutmeg

Heat apples over medium heat to boiling point; reduce heat, stirring occasionally, until tender, from 5 to 10 minutes. Stir in sugar, cinnamon, and nutmeg and heat to boiling. Remove from heat and put in jars.

PEANUT BUTTER SNACK

Ritz crackers
Peanut butter
Bark chocolate

Spread peanut butter between 2 Ritz crackers. Dip into melted bark chocolate. Cool on waxed paper.

BUTTERSCOTCH POPCORN

Microwave.

1 c. white corn syrup
2 (6 oz.) pkg.
  butterscotch
  chips
4 qt. popped corn
¾ c. peanut butter

Place corn syrup and butterscotch chips in a 1 quart measuring cup. Place cup in microwave oven and cook 4 to 5 minutes. Stir until smooth, then add peanut butter and stir again.

Place corn in a 5 quart dish or pan. Pour butterscotch syrup over corn, mixing evenly. Pour and press butterscotch popcorn into 13x9x2 inch dish or pan; refrigerate until set. Serve in squares or bars.

CARAMEL SAUCE

1 c. butter
3 c. firmly packed
  brown sugar
1 c. heavy cream

Combine butter and sugar over heat in heavy saucepan. Add cream. Boil 5 minutes without stirring. Beat 30 seconds or until foamy. Cool 3 to 5 minutes. Pour over ice cream.

ICE CREAM

4 pt. half & half
2 c. sugar
2 eggs, beaten
1 Tbsp. vanilla

Stir ingredients together. Refrigerate until cold. Put into ice cream maker and follow directions of ice cream maker to freeze. Makes 1 gallon of delicious ice cream.

EASY STRAWBERRY ICE CREAM

1 pkg. frozen
  strawberries
½ c. sugar
2 Tbsp. lemon juice
1 c. sour cream

Defrost and crush berries. Mix all ingredients well, then put in freezer tray and freeze 2 hours. Stir twice while freezing so ice cream will be smooth. Makes 4 servings.

CHOCOLATE DIPPED STRAWBERRIES

2 pt. strawberries
  (with stems)
1½ c. semi-sweet
  chocolate chips
2 Tbsp. corn syrup
5 to 9 Tbsp.
  margarine or
  butter

Wash strawberries. Pat dry. Place on paper towel until room temperature. Melt chocolate chips, corn syrup, and margarine in small saucepan over low heat. Stir occasionally. Remove from heat and set saucepan in pan of water to maintain dipping consistency. Dip each strawberry into chocolate mixture, coating ⅔ of strawberry. Allow excess to drip off. Place, stem side down, on waxed paper covered wire rack. Refrigerate until set, about 15 minutes.

INDEX OF RECIPES

BREADS, ROLLS, PASTRIES

DESSERTS

MISCELLANEOUS